the light through the shards

من تلك الشذرات انبثق الفجر

&

Alia Al-Sabi

Amany Khalifa

We have to start somewhere. The task at hand is not a simple one, and we have been stumbling around, trying to feel our way in the dark. What does it mean to write about refusal right now? This a question that unsettles us at a moment when we have been so thoroughly and effectively pushed to the extreme margins of existence. Let's spell things out lucidly: at the very moment that we are writing this, our people are undergoing genocide. The weight of this sentence plunges its fist down our throats and grips our hearts with a fury that makes it difficult to breathe.

1 2

7

We have to start somewhere. In torment, we turn inwards to our ancestral legacy of perseverance to find a light in the words and acts of those who came before us, so that we may not stray from our path in this dark hour. The project of genocide is not novel or recent, we know this. We've always known this. But the velocity and nefariousness of this phase of annihilation has hit with a meteoric force, designed to institute defeat in us, to stun us into paralysis. We write because it is one antidote to despair. Because writing has always been at the heart of our struggle, as part of a long lineage of revolutionary thought that perpetually ignites our collective spirit.

What transpired from this co-writing experiment is a stream of broken thoughts and words inspired by a long line of mentors: from our martyrs to our fighters, our poets and writers, our mothers, our friends, and our teachers. Informed by much of their guiding words for survival and liberation, this is a text that insists on "formal instability"[1] in the sense that, at times, it might feel elusive and fragmented, not because we necessarily intended for it to be so, but because we were often confronted by the impossibility of expressing with full comprehensibility.

1.
Edward W. Said, *After the Last Sky: Palestinian Lives.* (New York: Columbia University Press, 1999), 6, 38.

In which past tense becomes interchangeable with present tense and the linearity of thought is continuously disrupted, sometimes infused with an unavoidable futurity.

In which voices sometimes crowd together on a page, only to give way to complete silence.

In which words simply fail.

At times, we found the act of writing, a process that innately demands slowness, to be counterintuitive. The speed with which a drone can claim the lives of hun-dreds speaks to a technology of violence that exceeds our ability to comprehend it, let alone write about it. Through the ensuing correspondence we held over weeks and months, we tried to stay true to our anguish and our insistence to keep fighting, to keep writing from the dark corners of this horrific episode of our existence.

As such, it is an incomplete text.

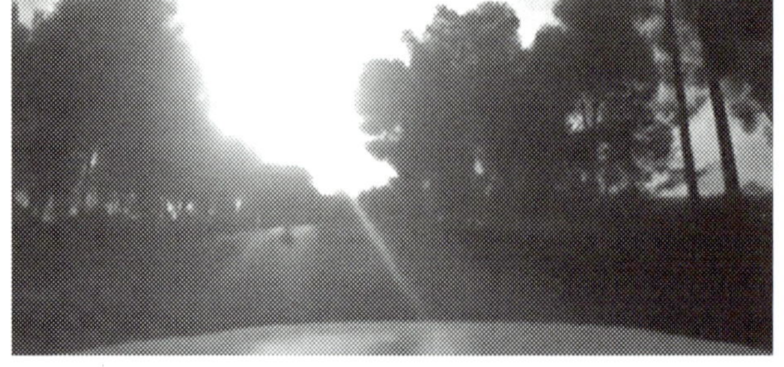

Lately, we've been reading Ghassan Kanafani's works as literary puzzles that demand some degree of decoding. The other day, we were talking about "Returning to Haifa," and one passage in particular, a cryptic and striking passage on return, compelled us to stop and sit with it. In the novella, Saeed tells Safiyeh:

> *"You know, for twenty long years I always imagined that the Mandelbaum Gate*[2] *would be opened some day, but I never, never imagined that it would be opened from the other side. It never entered my mind. So when they were the ones to open it, it seemed to me frightening and absurd and to a great degree humiliating. Maybe I'd be crazy if I told you that doors should always open from one side only, and that if they opened from the other side they must still be considered closed. But nevertheless, that's the truth."*[3]

Something about the fact that Saeed and Safiyeh were able to return to Haifa from Ramallah through this gate because they were "allowed" to, is what Ghassan is warning us against. It's a question not just of return itself, but also about the manner in which we return. This is what we're compelled to think about in this correspondence.

2.
Former checkpoint between the Israeli-occupied and Jordanian-occupied sides of Jerusalem before 1967. We really wanted to understand what Ghassan meant by this, right? So maybe let's just think about it for a moment. The door he was referring to, of course ,was the Mandelbaum Gate, which was destroyed after the Naksa in 1967 by the Israelis.

3.
Ghassan Kanafani. *Palestine's Children: Returning to Haifa and Other Stories: Returning to Haifa & Other Stories*, trans. Barbara Harlow and Karen E. Riley (Boulder: Lynne Rienner Publishers, 2000)

For the past week, I have been trying in many different ways to respond to your invitation, to begin with "return." I should have kept all the drafts I wrote over and over again; perhaps only by sharing them could I convey how daunting the task is. I feel as if I'm torn at every moment when I dig deep into my memory and begin to trace the minor details of the

obour,

passage.

That day in October,

Palestinians in Gaza opened the door from the only side possible, in Ghassan's formulation. And yet, it is crucial to reflect on this moment of epic passage, for it is one that simultaneously brought us closer to and shrouded our path from return. I'm sorry, I don't mean to sound defeatist. I want us to continue with this thread of thoughts, but I can't promise that I will not show the wounded and the scarred. I want them to be a testament to our journey with return. As we embark on this writing endeavor, taking the moment of that day in October as our departure, it is crucial to think of the tensions, the inconsistencies, and the multiplicity of meanings. And when Ghassan speaks of the "how" of return, the agony, the pain, the destruction, the broken and amputated limbs—these are all a part of this conversation.

Let's slow down a little and try to sit with the magnitude of what we are trying to articulate. That day in October changed all of our lives, I think forever. I remember exactly where I was—I had just woken up and found countless messages from you on my phone. We were in different time zones and you hadn't slept as the news started emerging by the break of dawn. I think I went out and sat in the sun to absorb what was happening. Somehow I needed the certainty of its light, and its warmth on my skin to ground myself in the moment, to believe

I was not dreaming.

Do you remember how you felt? It's like many years have passed since then, so much has happened. And we are *still* in the middle of waking up and sleeping to news of slaughters in Gaza every single day. Later on, I would look at footage, ones taken after the siege was broken, and I would look for the sun. It is the same one I was looking at in those same moments, far away from home.

But when you said that on that day in October, Palestinians opened the door—a moment that rendered us both closer and more distanced from return—what did you mean? To some extent, I think I understand. The breaking of the siege was followed by a brutal and vicious campaign of accelerated genocide, perpetrated by our colonizers, that rendered Gaza destroyed beyond recognition, and claimed the lives of thousands upon thousands of our people. In the face of our insurmountable loss, return seems beyond reach, even when we recognize the immensity of the act of passage that fateful morning. But there's a seeming contradiction in the dual temporality, the simultaneous distance and proximity from return. Take, for example, the moment that bulldozer charged forward, breaking the siege. Where would we locate that moment? To me, it appears like a hinge,

like a pivot
that exists to separate time into
what was before and what came after.

And like a hinge,
that moment
either furiously swivels us forward into an unclear future, or lunges us back into ground zero of the colonial violence that took root in our lands. No, not even that. Somehow, in that moment, we were collectively expelled from the sphere of time into the orbit of return, that ever-present realm where we all gather always at once. It is a paradoxical space in which we are always moving forward to go back. A realm that has been constituted since our mass expulsion decades ago, in which we inhabit an existential space that operates under a different temporality where past, present, and future are always intertwined indefinitely.

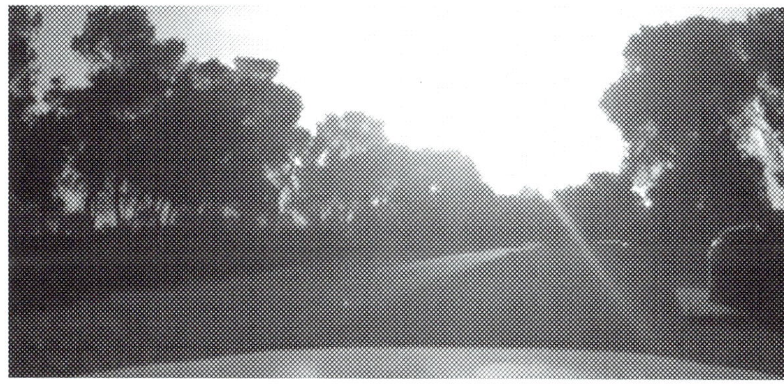

I don't know if this makes any sense.
Let me try again.

Do you know how we, the Palestinians, always speak of return as a movement where we imagine going back to the continuity of our lands and our lives as they were before 1948? It is as if we exist in a time continuum where we know time is moving forward but somehow, it is moving towards that time in the past, when our geographies were not fragmented and you could take a train from Haifa to Beirut. How do we reconcile the contradiction here? Moving forward to go back in time? This is why I keep returning to the metaphor of an orbit. The orbit of return as a loop

we move

forward

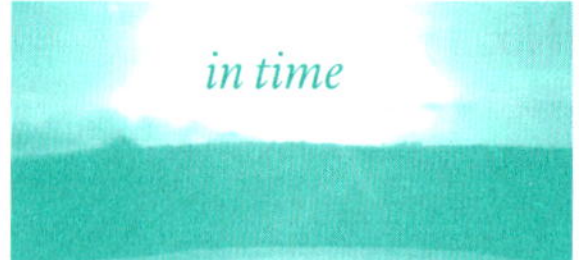

in order

to go back into space.

I know this is counterintuitive and defies fundamental logic, but we're not operating in the realm of rationale right now, we're trying to work out our movement across time and space in a way that retains the integrity of our struggle. This is an exercise in radical imagination, where we inhabit this extraterrestrial, extratemporal loop as a rehearsal for a return worthy of our collective sacrifice. It's a metaphysical conundrum because we don't adhere to universal laws that dictate we "moved on," both literally through the passage of time, but also condescendingly, in the admonishing voice of might over right.

It may help to imagine things visually. In my mind, the orbit of return looks like Earth's cycle around the sun, with our lives revolving daily around motions of return. It's all these things we do, every day.

Like smuggling into the '48 on ordinary days,
or the Great March of Return,
or reclaiming stolen archives,
or Shireen's[4] funeral,
when thousands of Palestinians swarmed the Hebron Gate, and Jerusalem was liberated, even if just for a day[5]—these ephemeral moments of liberation are also a part of the daily cycles of return.

4. Shireen Abu Akleh, who was killed by Israeli snipers while covering an army raid on the Jenin Refugee Camp on May 11, 2022.

5. Ali Habiballah, "In Farewell to Shireen…Jaffa Gate is Born Again," *Metras*, May 13, 2022. https://shorturl.at/ld9ph

This orbit is where we meet our grandparents when they were young, where our children will come and meet us. Motions of return exist between the imaginary and the tangible, and we are constantly moving between these states, however fleetingly. That day in October moved us from the realm of the symbolic to that of possibility, and that split second opened up the potential for new horizons and a different world. It was essentially an opening from the only side possible, the side that refuses capitulation to the occupiers' attempts to control our time and space. That alone is monumental.

The side that refuses capitulation. It is an important distinction, especially as we consider the conceptual and material devices that are essential for the sustenance of our return, the necessary components traversing this orbit we speak of. Although, I do not intend to portray a definitive and narrow sense of what return is. What I take from Ghassan's protagonist Saeed, however, is how critical the act of refusal is to the notion of return. Ghassan presents an affirmative rejection of gates opening by way of negotiations and submissions guised as peace treaties. This visceral sense of refusal is embedded in Ghassan's use of language when Saeed says: *"So when they were the ones to open it, it seemed to me frightening and absurd and to a great degree humiliating."* This line reminds me of *"ala'aideen"* (the returnees), the Palestinians who returned with Yasser Arafat as part of the Oslo Accords in 1994.[6] This was an event in our history that complicated the notion of return, as it was a byproduct of political submission. What we are saying is that not all returns are created equal. If we posit that a return facilitated by our oppressor and contingent on our submission is not a return we wish to enact,[7] then we must be unflinching in pursuing a return that is worthy of our people and the sacrifices they have made over time.

6.
of returnees is estimated at between 40 and 100 thousand Palestinians who surrendered by disbanding the Palestinian Liberation Movement, abandoning the struggle for liberation, and substituting both for the project of State-building under the premise of the Palestinian Authority.

When we say refusal, what we usually mean is the political stance we take that is rooted in a system of beliefs and conventions that follow what we hold to be logical and reasonable. And yet, the instances of refusal that we keep returning to contain something else. To be clear, we're not talking about the normative gestures of refusal such as boycotts in these instances, but the more fleeting and largely daring moments that truly define our history, such as breaking the siege. We spoke time and again about the ability of these moments to touch and transform us, for they are illogical, incomprehensible, and exceptional. I'm trying to tease out what else is at play here because I know, I feel, that there's a specificity to refusal that needs to be fleshed out.

7.
And in fact, guided by Ghassan, we should even go as far as to say that it is a form of return that nullifies itself. That the door, even if open, is still closed.

I started writing to you with the assertion that refusal must exist on the orbit of return. But I am also filled with doubt. As though with each attempt to capture its essence, refusal slips and evades capture. So when you asked me one time about the difference between refusal and resistance, I have to admit now that I don't know. It is a difficult and provocative question, but since we are considering this writing exercise as a rehearsal, I will try to reflect on it with you.

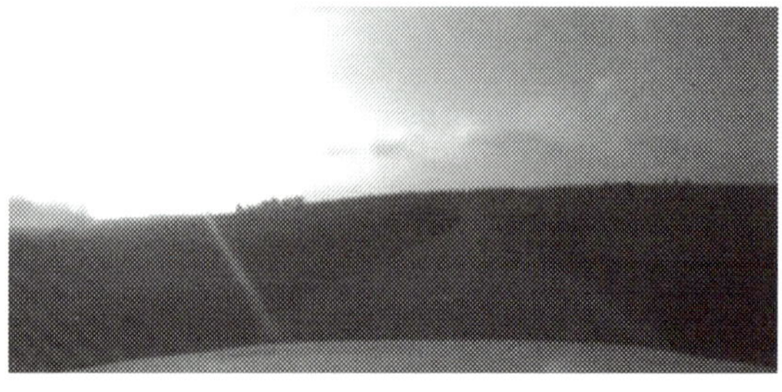

One way to think about it is to understand refusal as a resistant act that simultaneously shatters the status quo and opens up new horizons. It is neither passive nor reactionary. While with resistance, there is a component of survival embedded within the act that responds to the limitations of the present. And maybe refusal is distinct because it has a futuristic vision.[8] One refuses as long as one is aware of the possibility of making other choices. But listen, why go into this conceptual and abstract exercise? I always found concrete and tangible practices to be more exciting places to think from within.

8.
This is not to say that resistance and refusal are separate from one another – perhaps refusal can be seen as a subset of resistance that has a more specific charge.

Let me try again. I'm in conversation here with martyr, former[9] prisoner, and intellectual Walid Daqqah, through one of his more recent texts, "Al Saytara Bil Zaman" (Domination of Time)[10], where he tries to grasp and convey why a political prisoner would decide to go on hunger strike. Such a decision, Walid writes in astonishment, contradicts the laws and logic of the mind, for why would you subject your body to suffering in your struggle for a better life? He then surmises that his astonishment is derived from analytical logic, or pragmatism if you wish, and other calculations of feasibility.

9.
I hate interjecting like this, but Walid is still imprisoned. His body is still held by his Zionist captors, who refuse to release it to his family so they can bury and grieve him properly, until he finishes his sentence next year. Such is the brutal practice we call the Cemetery of Numbers.

10.
Walid Daqqah, "Domination with Time," *Awan*, June 16, 2021 https://www.awanmedia.net/article/6046

For the prisoners and those who engage in such debilitating endeavors, there is something else at play, what Walid calls "*mantiq a'qlani,*" which goes beyond what we know to be reasonable and rational to include the heart, body, and soul. He writes,

> *"'mantiq a'qlani' does not acknowledge the calculations of the mind that establish reality, nor does it change it. Rather, it takes objective reality and elevates it, and their rationality* ***refuses***[11] *to descend to reality and remain there. But descending to rise to higher ranks. This "'mantiq a'qlani" includes moral, ethical, humanitarian, and national considerations, as well as individual values of the self, which transform the mind, body, and heart into more than a mechanical sum of parts".*

↑
(This passage puzzles me.)

11.
Emphasis added by us.

How is a hunger-striking prisoner's logic of subjecting one's body to starvation a form of "descending to rise to higher ranks," as Walid says? Disappeared from the surface of the land and the fabric of their society, our prisoners exist under the brute locus of power with every concentration of violence possible rained mercilessly on them, sometimes indefinitely. In the most confined space of incarceration, where the imprisoned are stripped of all and every element of control, the body becomes the last frontier of resistance and the final corpus of control. And so, every resistant act that a prisoner commits, no matter how small, takes on a magnitude of larger proportions. The degradation of the body in protest elevates the act of resistance; it is an act of refusal that contains a life and soul-sustaining force because it works to preserve the wholeness of the prisoner's spirit as a colonized subject even as his body withers away.

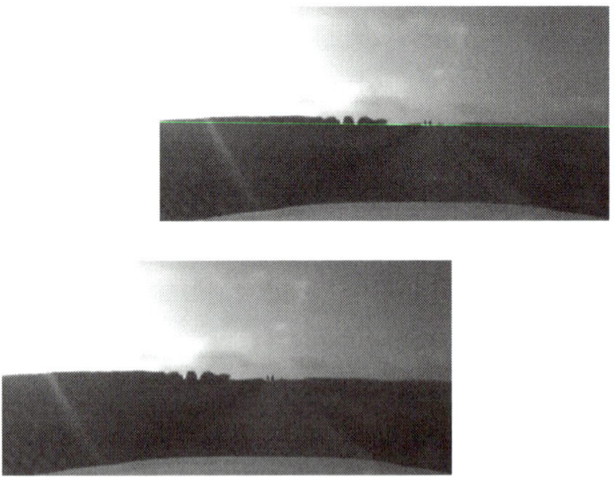

I think this is what Walid means by the kind of logic that rejects normative calculations of sense and practicality. To understand refusal not as a reactionary stance, but as a rejection of passivity, even, and especially if we are ultimately still killed in the end. It is a core element that fundamentally recognizes the existential war waged upon us, and then mobilizes us to completely reject the terms and conditions that ultimately prolong our annihilation. Our history of resistance is filled to the brim with endless formulations of such refusal.

When a man sits atop the rubble of his house drinking tea and smoking *nargileh*, we recognize his symbolic act as both a defiance and negation of zionist rule over our time and space. To the onlooker, the man is sitting over rubble but to us, to him, it is his home over his land, which he will rebuild, again and again, no matter how many times he has to do it. That is quintessential refusal.

It's necessary, then, to view the breaking of the siege on that day in October in this light—as part of a long trajectory of resistance that has always labored to carve out our own terms and conditions, our own space and time, our own song and dance. That moment of rupture encompasses both return and refusal in its essence. It was both a refusal to surrender to the decades-long siege imposed on Gaza, facilitated by a world order that deemed our lives less valuable, and a form of return in both its literal and metaphorical sense.[12] If we were to map this moment on the orbit of return, it would be seen not as a break from the path but an intensified movement that pulls us closer to the core of our struggle. There is the sun, and we moved that much closer to it that day.

12. This refusal didn't begin on that day in October, and it didn't end there. Think of the thousands of families who refused to leave their homes in northern Gaza for fear of repeating the tragedy of the Nakba. Also, I think of the Great March of Return in 2018 and also then Gazanes declared their refusal of being refugees and insisted on having the right to access their homes and their land in which they have been displaced from in 1948.

Speaking of rotations around the sun and movements towards return, I want to share something that's been on my mind as we've been deliberating on meanings and acts of refusal. May 15, 2011, marking the 63rd Nakba, was and will be remembered as a pivotal day in our collective memory. Protesting their prolonged exile, thousands of Palestinian refugees swarmed the borders of occupied Palestinian land. Some marched from the Syrian border to the village of Majdal Shams in the occupied Golan Heights—five refugees were shot dead by Zionist snipers, and a few others were unexpectedly able to cross the imposed border and reach the occupied village. On the Lebanese side, we witnessed a similar movement, where protesting refugees gathered in the village of Maroun El Ras and attempted to cross into Palestine. Ten protestors were killed by occupation forces in the process.

That same day in Amman and Cairo, hundreds of protesters took to the streets to demand the implementation of the right of return. And in Palestine, the heart of it all, I remember in detail the mass protests across the land, with groups of demonstrators flocking to the northern border with Lebanon, and others marching in Haifa, Jerusalem, Qalandia, Ramallah, and Gaza. I *return* to this day precisely because this is a moment in our history when we were able to disrupt Zionist narratives and temporality. The corporeal capacity of the refugees to march towards the borders of Palestine opened the door on our side and transformed our collective memory as well as the notion of return from the symbolic to the material realm. It also brought the political horizon of liberation within reach.

All this is to say that we cannot continue this conversation without devoting some space and attention to the significance of collective memory to the orbit of return. For Palestinians, a sacred bond exists between memory, existence, and ultimately return, which is why it is critical to trace and contemplate some of the historical and structural mechanisms embedded in this relation.

First—and I might sound overly simplistic, but bear with me—Palestinian historians, artists, literary scholars, and others have long been occupied with documenting our memory, retrieving the archive, and revealing the "truth." Such efforts aim, in large part, to counter the settler colonial narrative that denies our very existence and relationship to our homeland and justifies its colonial and expansionist project in Palestine. Temporally, the Nakba is almost always set as the point of departure for these endeavors. While this is an important task, it is crucial to bring to the surface the ways in which we approach the question of memory, mainly to avoid falling into the trap of settler colonial logics and frameworks of erasure.

Let me go back one step. When the Nakba becomes ground zero for our memories and stories of dispossession, when we cling to this moment as The Ultimate Event in our history, we inevitably succumb to the binary of defeat and victory. We surrender to the settler colonial linear timeline of beginnings and ends. We remain confined within the logic of loss, and we become perpetually immersed in a melancholic past. I believe this is why Walid said: *"I do not want to return to the Palestine of the past, the Mandatory Palestine of the cactus, the pomegranates, and the water mills, because it simply does not exist except in memory."*[13] This is not a negation of memory, it is a rejection of stagnancy and confinement of memory and time, especially when it is locked in mourning.

There is also another layer that demands our attention. When our existence is entirely occupied by a yearning for a past that has been lost, we in some ways internalize defeat. I'm thinking of Abdul Rahim Al-Shaikh and his refusal to read the Nakba as a moment of defeat. He's critical of this particular framing of the Nakba, because he understands it as a framework necessary to safeguard and nourish the Zionist project and the positioning of its inception as a victorious feat. More than anything, this historical view could obscure all the lasting and fleeting instances in which we were able to deform[14] the zionist settler colonial framework of time and space, such as that iconic day on May 15, 2011. These moments are the fuel to our imagination, mobilizing a different, more active, vision of return and liberation.

13.
Abdel Rahim Al-Sheikh, "The Parallel Space: Portraying Time in Walid Daqqah's Thought," *Majallat al-Dirasat al-Filastiniyya*, 135, (Summer 2023), https://www.palestine-studies.org/ar/node/1653995
.

14.
Abdaljawad Omar, "Bleeding Forms: Beyond the Intifada," *Critical Times*, March 14, 2024, https://shorturl.at/jRXRu. We're borrowing the notion of "deformation" from Abdel Jawad Omar's description of how events like Oct 7 deformed Zionist temporality and spatiality.

15.
Rana Barakat, "Ongoing Nakba, Ongoing return," published on *Jadaliyya* on March 14, 2024 https://www.jadaliyya.com/Details/45844

16.
Adam HajYahia, "The Principle of Return: the repressed rupture of the zionist time," *Parapraxis* on April 7, 2024 https://www.parapraxismagazine.com/articles/the-principle-of-return

When you said that the temporality of return exists in an ever-lasting present, this is true precisely because of how memory operates as a pivotal element in our political existence and struggle for liberation. In some ways, our insistence on memory is a form of returning to self, or more precisely, to the collective self. When we cite our predecessors, from our grandmothers to our poets to our martyrs, what we seek in their words is a rejoinder to move and keep moving, to defy stagnance. We enact motions of return from sites of history and memory, be they our fragmented lands or dispersed people. This approach to memory and history is what Rana Barakat calls the "ongoing return,"[15] a crucial method through which she invites us to anchor our return in belonging and love, insist on relationality to the land, and set our memory free of the confines of settler colonial frameworks—be they structural, temporal, and/or discursive. Rana's talk reminds me of this great line I read in Adam HajYahia's article[16] which speaks to questions of temporality, memory, and return, in which he writes that *"return produces possibility and fractures the apparatus that polices our imagination and our life. It is the opening to the future as endless uncaptured time..."*

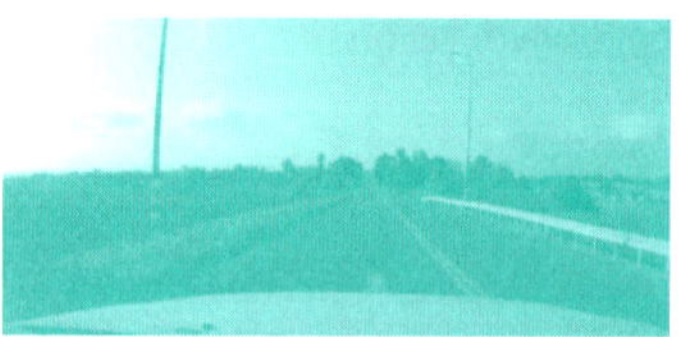

This is it, the idea of return as possibility. Also, thinking of it as an ongoing movement ensures that we do not fall prey to tired slogans and dusty cliches of what land and liberation mean to us. It is like the protagonist, Hamada, in Khaled Odetallah's "Returning to Yafa," who listens to his grandfather narrate the same stories of the Nakba every year, and finds himself bored. Here, I'm going to include a translated excerpt because Khaled really has a way with words,

"The grandfather's words vanished into the ether, but they slowly pushed Hamada's Nakba-heavy identity into lethargy every year. And in an instance of adventurous consciousness, Hamada began to peel away his "bereaved Palestinian-ness" like the ripe Jaffa oranges of his grandfather's stories, to discover as he was peeling his "Palestinian-ness" that he was also shedding at the same time, a hidden Zionist streak intertwined with it. For the idea of "Israel" had taken root in the rituals of the grieving mind. Nerve cells that enable consciousness to not be anything but its nemesis, so 'return' turned into everything contrary to the notion. It is the habit of the defeated to resort to abstraction after they have drowned in symbolism.

No longer was 'return' in Hamada's new cognitive system: a rusty key, an old land deed, a rhythmic poem or prose, a work of art, a ceremonial speech, black and white photos, or statistics and UNRWA archives. Instead, his disciplined athletic mind and his aversion to rhetoric compelled him to define 'return' in the language and technology of crossing borders as: types of barbed wire, systems of monitoring and surveillance, patrol schedules, drilling and cutting machinery, the art of camouflaging footstep traces, knowing road signs and smuggling nodes. Crossing the border preoccupied Hamada the Jaffan, of a Palestinian father and an Egyptian mother. The whole world before his eyes turned into a border that must be crossed."[17]

17. Khaled Odetallah (@kodetalah), "Returning to Yafa," *X.com*, May 15, 2024, https://encr.pw/yZ1yS

I read this short story so many times and lingered on this passage in particular because I recognized my own weariness with our tropes of return. How many more keys and how many more maps can we collectively hold? But also, I found that Hamada's own conversion of memory into a technology of return challenged my understanding of it. How many of us subconsciously hold entrenched ideas of the state's permanence and prowess, and therefore our own inevitable futility to dismantle it? I can't help but think of Hamada and his interpretation of the memory of the Nakba as the need to acquire technical knowledge – road signs and schedules and types of barbed wire. There's something really crucial here in this formula of memory as applied science; it's the activation of meaning through movement, both physical and conceptual, towards a tangible return.

→
18.
Hussein Mroue, "Fatal Grief and Fighting Grief," *Bab Elwad*, July 2, 2019, https://shorturl.at/PTq5y

I want us to sit with both Khaled and Ghassan's stories of returning. Ghassan's narration of Saeed's return is laced with remorse and fashioned as a precautionary tale as to which side the door opens to on our path of return. In Khaled's formulation, it is an acknowledgment of how internalized defeat produces a cliched narrative of return that is symbolic and frozen in a moment of time, and how that narrative is converted, in Hamada's consciousness, into a mode of acquiring technical knowledge that can facilitate actual return. Ghassan/Saeed and Khaled/Hamada are both speaking to moments in our history that mark our trajectory of struggle in different ways. Between Saeed's belief that *"doors should always open from one side only, and that if they opened from the other side they must still be considered closed"* and Hamada's belief that *"the whole world before his eyes turned into a border that must be crossed,"* what do you think has changed? Has anything changed?

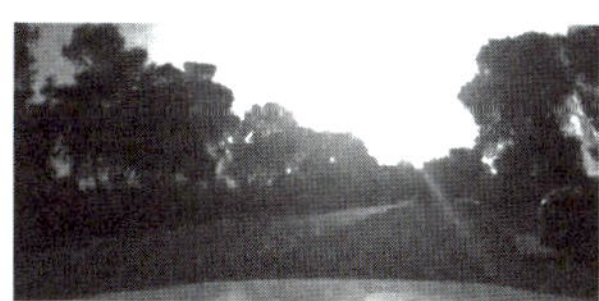

I'm afraid of losing sight. There are rivers of blood and mountains of rubble and flesh. Grief is air, at times still, invisible except for the fact of its existence. At times ferocious and unyielding, a cyclone of ache. Hussein Mroue once described grief in words that have remained with me -

"Your grief is the fatal kind. It kills you first, and it is, first and foremost, one of the murderers standing in enemy lines. It aims its bullets, psychologically and mentally, towards us in the battle of sumoud, now the pillar of our national struggle. But the grief of the young man standing his ground in that same battle, is the fighting kind. It is a sacred grief. It is the most beautiful, the most noble kind of great grief."[18]

A fatal grief,

a fighting grief,

a sacred grief,

and the worlds and universes

between them.

1 2

Why do you wake the world from its slumber?

**That sound isn't mine,*
it's the sound of my corpse hitting the ground.

And why don't you die silently?

**Because a silent death is a degraded life.*

And a bellowing one?

**Is a cause.*

Have you come to announce your presence?

**No, I came to declare my absence.*[19]

←
19.
We want to note here a lull in our conversation that lasted days and weeks. Our writing gradually came to a halt and our attempts to revive the momentum were stilted and unwieldy. So we stopped, and tried to take stock of what the writing process had generated thus far.

20.
Reading these words again as we receive news of the Al Mawassi massacre on July 13, today is one of those days. The reality of writing these words literally as a massacre unfolds…

There are days you wake up and read the day's tally of the dead and fall back into a pit of numbness, and there are days you wake up and you can't even exist in your body because the emotions are too monstrous to bear.[20] I'll be honest. In the past few weeks as we were corresponding, I felt myself dragging around. A lifelessness settled over our words and somehow nothing could shake the dead weight off. I noticed how we subconsciously hyper-focused on small details—I think it was a way of pushing through this eerie silence—until meaning disintegrated into incoherent fragments.

In this text, we tried to examine the logic of colonial violence, resistance, and refusal; how to think historically and how to imagine the future, how to trace the movement of return and the entanglement of its various elements, and how to center our legacies of practice and thought in our writing and forms of knowledge production. Yet inherent to this movement is an insurmountable reckoning that breaks you, and draws you into an unbearable state of being and an endless well of despair.

The reckoning here is the blood of our people, eclipsed momentarily by thoughts on orbits, refusal, and memory... before the dead once again asserted their absence and effectively forced us to stop and listen to the silences in our text. The vision of endless broken bodies and broken homes hovers over our heads and resides in our bones. I am struggling with this particular facet in our orbit of return. Our martyrs, so many of them. But not just that they're dead, that they're also viciously disfigured into unrecognizable fragments. The rubble, the flesh, the flesh in the rubble, and the rubble in the flesh. Collapsed onto one another, what is tissue and what is stone?

21. Mariam Mohammed Al Khateeb. "The Luxury of Death," *Institute for Palestine Studies,* June 10, 2024 https://palestine-studies.org/en/node/1655709 After typing this, I noticed how my body felt - a deep-seated nausea that has somehow become embedded in my gut that I don't even realize has turned into a semi-permanent state nowadays. A heavy metallic ball lodged in my core, rusting away.

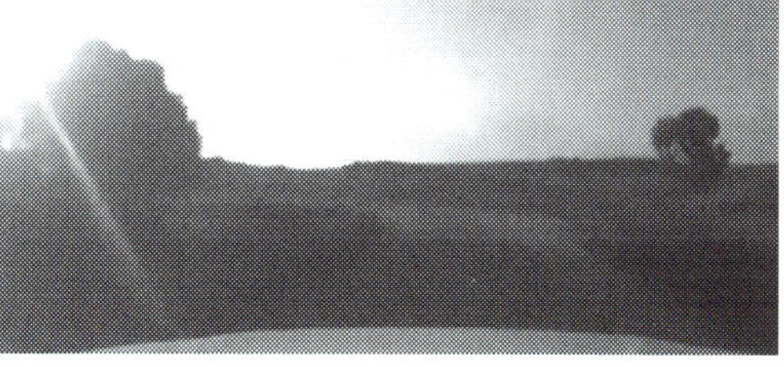

I am haunted by the words of Mariam Al-Khateeb, a poet from Gaza,where she writes:

"No one dies complete. After a missile strike, everyone searches in the debris to put their loved ones back together. Mothers search for their children's heads to match with their bodies. To be a good mother in the rest of the world is to feed your children good food and keep them warm, but to be a good mother in Gaza is to bury your children whole."[21]

My God, these words. The reckoning is not just the blood of our people, but their torn limbs and decapitated heads. "*The sound of my corpse hitting the ground,*" except the corpse has been indefinitely mutilated[22] and its declaration of absence is now split into many simultaneous screams. Infinite ruptures everywhere—we recount them so that we can begin to contain them in our limited cognition—bodies under the rubble, lineages exterminated, neighborhoods flattened, infrastructures and civil society relentlessly bombarded. We recount them so that we can begin to contain them. But the fissures are deep, and the voids are an abyss that refuses containment. The absences are not one, they are endless. To sit with these fissures, this emptiness. To carry them with us, our dead as they assert their absence, is at the heart of it all.

I think what you're saying here is that we need to envision a different kind of movement. We've been talking about the orbit of return as though our struggle exists within an ordered, repetitive pattern. But what if, instead of pushing for some sort of rationale to close or contain the gaps, we think of a movement that emerges from within the fractures and the fragments that define our current reality. I'm thinking of that concluding passage in Ghassan's "Letter to Gaza," where he says,

> *"My friend ... Never shall I forget Nadia's leg, amputated from the top of the thigh. No! Nor shall I forget the grief which had molded her face and merged into its traits forever. I went out of the hospital in Gaza that day, my hand clutched in silent derision on the two pounds I had brought with me to give Nadia. The blazing sun filled the streets with the colour of blood. And Gaza was brand new, Mustafa! You and I never saw it like this. The stone piled up at the beginning of the Shujaiya quarter where we lived had a meaning, and they seemed to have been put there for no other reason but to explain it. This Gaza in which we had lived and with whose good people we had spent seven years of defeat was something new. It seemed to me just a beginning. I don't know why I thought it was just a beginning. I imagined that the main street that I walked along on the way back home was only the beginning of a long, long road leading to Safad. Everything in this Gaza throbbed with sadness which was not confined to weeping. It was a challenge: more than that it was something like reclamation of the amputated leg!"*[23]

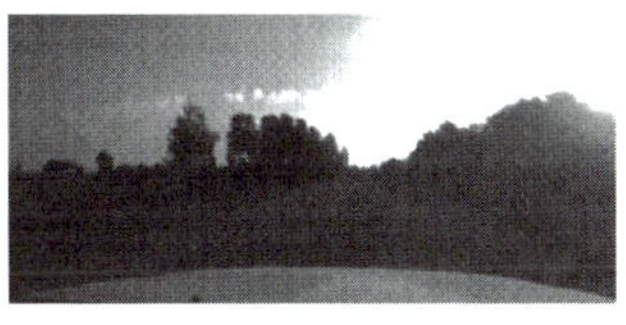

←
22.
I am haunted by the word أشلاء, how there is no word in English that can capture the violence of the killing.

23.
Ghassan Kanafani, "Letter from Gaza," published in translation into English in The 1936-39 Revolt in Palestine by the Tricontinental Society of London in 1980. This text was written in the context of the Israeli invasion of Gaza and the Khan Yunis and Rafah massacres in November, 1956.

It's as if Ghassan was anticipating the moment we are living when he wrote this passage. There's a crucial image that he's drawing here— the ontological path that begins from Gaza and persists until it reclaims the amputated leg. Something about this line that he draws between the long road that begins in Gaza and leads to Safad as a movement akin to a reclamation of a severed leg must be instructive for us in this moment rife with so many of us broken and maimed. Imagine a march of return, with many of us on crutches, with prosthetic limbs, moving slowly, disjointedly, imperfectly but still moving together—this I think, is the work of moving within the fissure. Still, I want us to remain a little longer with the absences and how they suffocate us. Because we can't bring the dead back and we are forced under conditions of imposed separation to witness our genocide from degrees of distance, where writing becomes a medium to express, yes, the debility we feel, but also our deep anguish and desire to hold our people close, to hold one another.

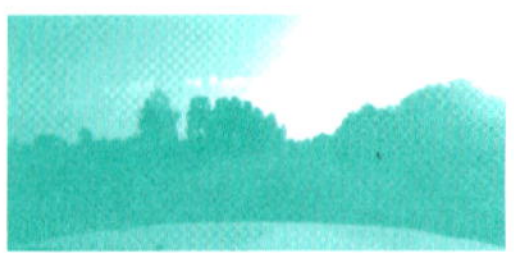

"I wish my eye was a river, mother, so they can drink from it" I have been humming these words to myself for the past ten months, almost unconsciously. Like a lullaby, as if to soothe an ache. "*I wish my body was a bridge, mother, so they can cross it.*"[24] And what words can soothe the ache of an amputated limb or a loved one killed? None. I wish I could embrace every father who has lost his child, and every child who has lost her mother. That's the feeling, a suffocated desire to touch, to hold them. In the impossibility to do so, I wish I could at least write touch. Infuse touch into language, but how? Hypatia said that "*we must touch and be touched by language to be in the world.*"[25] Right now there is no world outside of Gaza, and we are not there. So how can language be the vehicle to bring us closer?

24.
William Nassar. "A'la Tariq Aitat," July 20, 2013. https://www.youtube.com/watch?v=KbOnbjyDgxc.

25.
Vourloumis, Hypatia. "Ten theses on touch, or, writing touch." *Women & Performance: a journal of feminist theory 24,* no. 2-3 (2014): 232-238.

I think what Hypatia is alluding to is a political commitment to how we inhabit the world. This is a modality where language becomes a medium in which we insist on living in contradiction to what structures of power deem acceptable for us. This is why I refuse to submit to the dominant logics of and universal laws of the world. And why we speak of extraterrestrial, extratemporal orbits and revolutions around the sun. We are roaming in unfamiliar terrain, exploring possibilities that exist in the space of banishment we have been expelled to. I'm thinking of the importance of touch in language — it goes beyond abstraction and insists on the concrete, like the essence of touch is that you can feel it, it's not a metaphor. It can be embodied in the details of things, for instance. Like when you describe the temperature of the sun, how it feels on your skin, its immediacy on your body. Touch in language is also to be attentive, careful, concerned, and loving. It is a refusal of individuation; one touches and is touched, and in that process the cycle of isolation breaks. The significance of touch lies in its ability to summon and compel us to experience and feel communally. Or as Fred Moten and Stefano Harney would say, *"Though forced to touch and be touched, to sense and be sensed in that space of no space, though refused sentiment, history and home, we feel (for) each other."*[26] In that space of no space, be it the slave ship crossing the Atlantic, or the space of exclusion formed when the violence of colonial borders clamps down on us with a brute force that disperses us into all corners of the earth, how do "we feel (for) each other"? And why is this important, even fundamental for our survival as a people? Fred and Stefano call this mode of feeling hapticality, or *"the capacity to feel through others, for others to feel through you, for you to feel them feeling you, this feel of the shipped is not regulated, at least not successfully, by a state, a religion, a people, an empire, a piece of land, a totem."*[27] This realm of touch through language, through the capacity to feel, in which we can exist and forge sensorial and embodied relationships with our people, whom we love but cannot physically embrace, is a radical realm precisely because it defies the regulation of power. In that remaining space of

26.
Stefano Harney and Fred Moten, "The Undercommons: Fugitive planning and black study." (New York: Minor Compositions, 2013): 98-99.

27.
Ibid.

uncontrolled sensorial presence, we must insist on finding alternate practices to overcome our separation and sense of alienation, so as not to surrender to the distance established upon us. Perhaps these propositions seem incoherent and detached.

↑

(The other day, after the Al-Mawassi massacre, a man said *"I hid my children from the sun the whole way, and when we arrived, they struck them dead."*)

↓

I'm not sure how to proceed from here. All I can think of is the sea of fractures we are engulfed in and the question of how we can survive this annihilation. At the heart of thinking of sense and touch as imaginative practices that can aid us in this moment is a desperation to not succumb to the numbing pain as an inevitable graveyard where all our senses go to die, but instead, to convert the grief into a sustained tension that we can never resolve. A fire that we can never extinguish. That is the sacred, fighting grief.

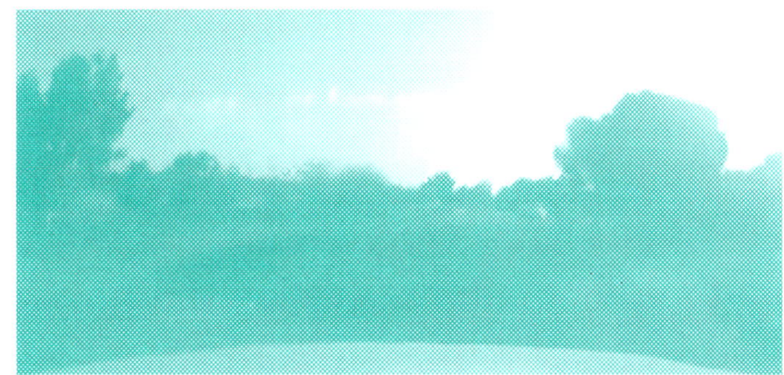

Yet, we must acknowledge the distance that separates us, the safety it yields us, and even the fact of the privilege of writing these very words. This is an admission of responsibility. It is impossible to find the right words, or just any words. This is why this text will always be incomplete. And now that we're here, at the tail end of our correspondence. It has become clear that the vision that we initially had, of the orbit of return, is also broken. Not because the pathways of return we conceived of don't work, but because they don't function in this perfectly cyclical science like planets do. The components are all there—refusal, memory, sacrifice, grief—but they don't always move in unison nor are they formulaic elements that coalesce into a comprehensive whole. No, where the orbit is sealed in a perfectly determined pathway, our own journey of return is jagged, with sharp edges and ruptures, deep chasms and detonated roads, lined with the bodies of our martyrs and the limbs of our maimed, of years spent in prison cells and held up at checkpoints. Where the orbit is locked in a recurring cycle, its planets organized along a fixed route that does not veer from its passage, our movement of return is unpredictable and subject to improvisation. Not a sum of logical parts, because it has its own mode of *mantiq a'qlani'*, as Walid would say. And yet, to say it is unpredictable is not to say that it lacks certainty. On the contrary, we are certain of return even though it defies the logic of power, or the "facts on the ground." We are certain of it like the certainty of the sun, of its sight, and its warmth on our skin. Like that day, in the early morning, when the world over held its breath as the news started unfolding.

Do you remember how you felt? The sun seemed so bright, and it kept getting brighter and brighter, warming our souls before it started burning us with its touch.

من تلك الشذرات انبثق الفجر

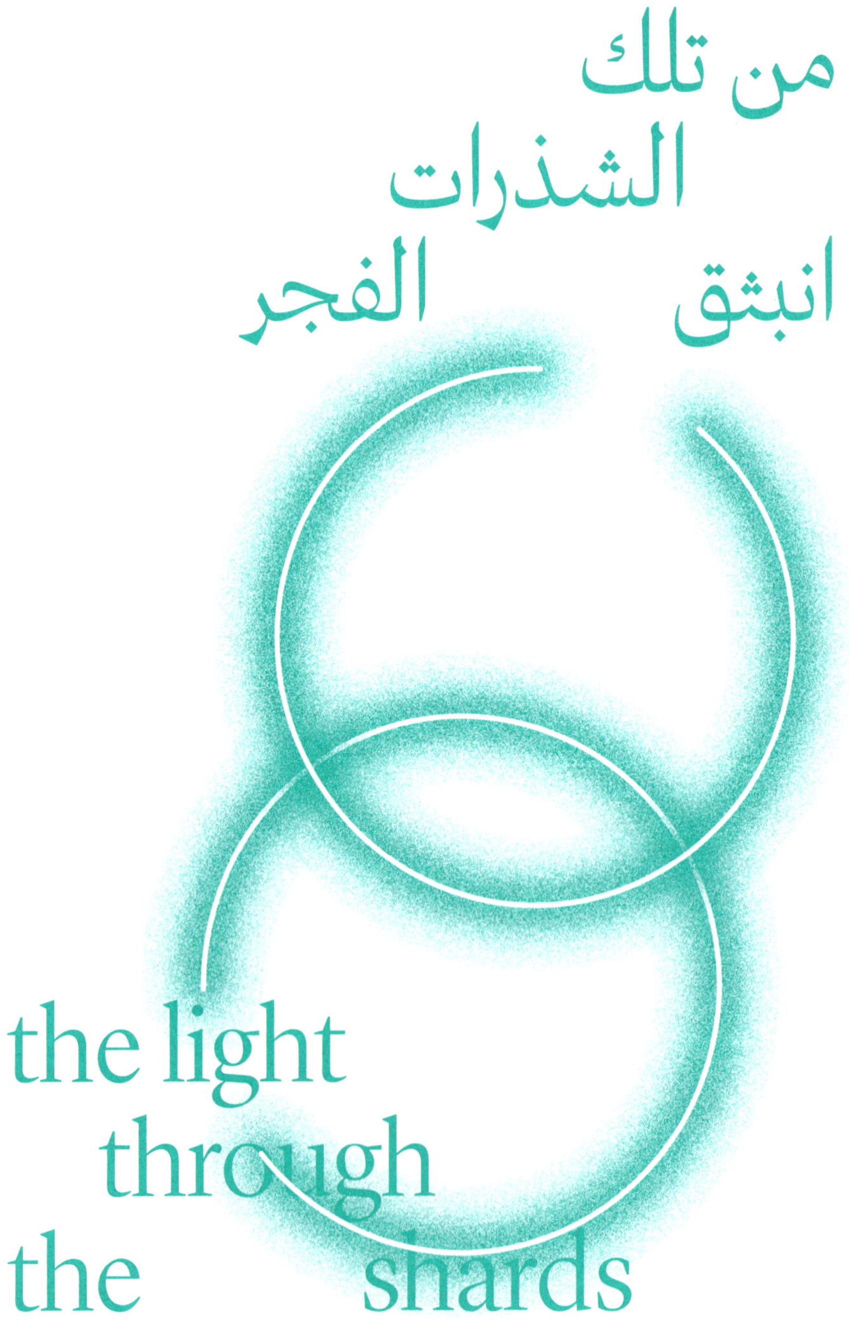

the light through the shards

علياء السبع و أماني خليفة

٤

علينا أن نبدأ من مكان ما، إذ إنّ المهمّة الملقاة على عاتقنا ليست سهلة، نتخبّط ونتعثّر، محاولين أن نشقّ طريقنا في الظلام. ماذا نعني أن نكتب عن الرفض في هذه اللحظة؟ يربكنا هذا السؤال في الوقت الذي نُدفع فيه إلى أقصى هوامش الوجود. لنضع النقاط على الحروف: في هذه اللحظة الّتي نكتب فيها، يتعرّض شعبنا للإبادة. إنّ ثقل هذه الجمل يخترق حناجرنا ويعصر قلوبنا ويخنقها.

٢ ١

٦

٧

١ ٢

علينا أن نبدأ من مكان ما. وسط كلّ هذه المعاناة، نلتفت إلى إرث أجدادنا، لنستمدّ منه صمودًا نستضيء به، من كلمات وأفعال كلّ من سبقونا، حتّى لا نحيد عن الطريق في أحلك اللحظات. نحن نعلم أنّ مشروع الإبادة الجماعيّة ليس جديدًا، ولطالما عرفنا ذلك، ولكنّ سرعة وفظاعة هذه المرحلة من الإبادة ضربتنا بقوّة ساحقة، إذ صُمّمت لزرع الهزيمة فينا وشلّنا بشكل تامّ. نكتب، لأنّ الكتابة علاج لليأس، ولأنّ فعل الكتابة متجذّر في صلب نضالنا، كجزء هامّ من إرثنا الثوريّ الطويل الّذي يشعل روحنا الجماعيّة باستمرار.

تجربة الكتابة المشتركة هذه، نتج عنها سيل من الأفكار والكلمات المتناثرة المستوحاة من سلسلة طويلة من المرشدين؛ شهداؤنا ومناضلونا، شعراؤنا وكتّابنا، أمّهاتنا، أصدقاؤنا وصديقاتنا، ومعلّمونا. مستندين على أقوالهم حول البقاء والتحرّر، يصرّ هذا النصّ على "اللا-استقرار الشكليّ"،[1] بمعنى أنّه قد يبدو في بعض الأحيان غامضًا ومتشتّتًا، لا لأنّنا قصدنا ذلك بالضرورة، وإنّما لأنّنا واجهنا استحالة وصعوبة في التعبير.

١. إدوارد سعيد، ما بعد السماء الأخيرة: حياة الفلسطينيين. (نيويورك: مطبعة جامعة كولومبيا، ١٩٩٩)،٦، ٣٨.

١٠

يتداخل الماضي مع الحاضر، وينقطع تسلسل أفكارنا باستمرار، وأحيانًا، تتخلّل النصّ لمحات من مستقبل حتميّ.

على هذه الصفحات، تتزاحم أصواتنا، لتفسح المجال للصمت.

حين تخذلنا الكلمات.

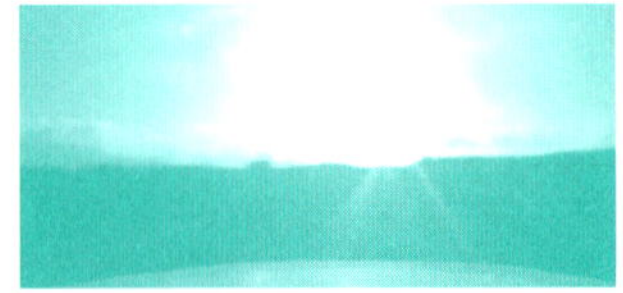

في بعض الأحيان، وجدنا أنّ فعل الكتابة الّذي يحتاج بطبيعته إلى البطء، أصبح خيارًا غير منطقيّ، في مقابل السرعة الّتي تمكّن طائرة مسيّرة من قتل مئات الأرواح، والّتي بدورها تدلّل على تكنولوجيا عنف تتجاوز قدرتنا على إدراكها، فماذا عن الكتابة عنها؟ لذلك، ومن خلال المراسلات الّتي تبادلناها على مدار الأسابيع والشهور، حاولنا أن نبقى وفيّتين وصادقتين تجاه آلامنا، ومصرّتين على مواصلة هذا النضال بكافّة أشكاله، والاستمرار بالكتابة عنه من زوايا هذه المرحلة المُعتمة من وجودنا.

وبالتّالي، فإنّ هذا النصّ غير مكتمل.

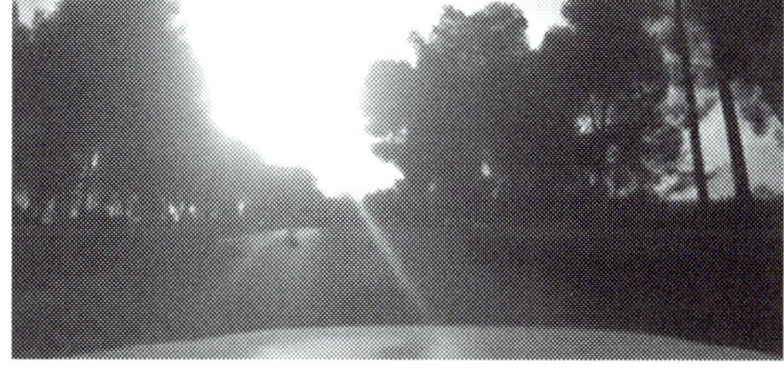

في الآونـة الأخيـرة، كنّا نقرأ أعمـال غسّان كنفاني كألغاز أدبيّة تستدعي منّا بعض الجهد لتفكيكها. وقبل أيّام، تحدّثنا حول رواية 'عـائد إلى حيفا'، وكانت هناك فقرة معيّنة غامضة ومثيرة تتحدّث عن مفهوم العودة، استوقفتنا هذه الفقـرة ودعتنا للتأمّل، إذ يقول سعيد لصفيّة:

"أتعرفين؟ طوال عشرين سنة كنت أتصوّر أنّ بوّابة مندلبوم[٢] *ستفتح ذات يوم... ولكن أبدًا، أبدًا لم أتصوّر أنّها ستفتح من الناحية الأخرى. لم يكن ذلك يخطر لي على بال، ولذلك فحين فتحوها هم، بدا لي الأمر مرعبًا وسخيفًا وإلى حدّ كبير مهينًا تمامًا... قد أكون مجنونًا لو قلت لك إنّ كلّ الأبواب يجب ألّا تُفتح إلّا من جهة واحدة، وأنّها إذا فُتحت من الجهة الأخرى، فيجب اعتبارها مغلقة لا تزال، ولكنّ تلك هي الحقيقة".*[٣]

٢.
نقطة التفتيش السابقة بين الجانب الذي احتلّته إسرائيل والجانب الذي خضع للوصاية الأردنيَة من القدس قبل عام ١٩٦٧. أردنا حقًّا أن نفهم ما الذي كان يعنيه غسّان بذلك؟ دعونا نفكّر فيه قليلًا. إنّ البوَابة التي كان يتحدث عنها هي بالتأكيد بوّابة مندلبوم التي دمّرها الإسرائيليّون بعد نكسة الـ١٩٦٧.

٣.
غسّان كنفاني، أطفال فلسطين: عائد إلى حيفا وقصص أخرى، ترجمة باربارا هارلو وكارين إي. رايلي، بولدر: دار نشر لين رينر، ٢٠٠٠.

يحاول غسّان أن يحذّرنا من فكرة أنّ سعيد وصفيّة استطاعا العودة إلى حيفا من رام الله عبر هذه البوّابة؛ لأنّه "سُمِح لهم" بذلك. وبالتّالي، فإنّ المسألة هنا غير متعلّقة بفعل العودة نفسه، وإنّما في الطريقة الّتي يمكن أن نعود من خلالها. هذا ما سنحاول التفكير به في هذه المراسلات. ١٣

طوال الأسبوع الماضي، حاولت الردّ على دعوتك هذه بطرق مختلفة، والبدء من مفهوم "العودة". كان عليّ الاحتفاظ بكلّ تلك المسوّدات الّتي كتبتها مرارًا وتكرارًا؛ وأعتقد أنّني ومن خلال مشاركتها، سأتمكّن من إيصال مدى صعوبة هذه المهمّة، وكم أتمزّق في كلّ مرّة أعود فيها إلى ذاكرتي للبدء بتتبّع تفاصيل

في ذلك اليوم من شهر أكتوبر، فتح الفلسطينيّون في غزّة الباب من الجهة الوحيدة الممكنة وفقًا لتصوّر غسّان. ومع ذلك، من الضروريّ أن نتأمّل في لحظة العبور العظيم. لأنّها اللحظة الّتي قرّبتنا من طريق العودة، وحجبته عنّا في الوقت نفسه. أعتذر. لا أقصد أن أبدو انهزاميّة. أريد أن نستمرّ في تسلسل أفكارنا، ولكنّني لا أملك أيّ ضمانات بأنّني لن أظهر هشاشتي وجروحي، بل العكس تمامًا، أريد لهذه الندوب أن تشهد على رحلة عودتنا. بينما نتّخذ لحظة ذلك اليوم من أكتوبر نقطة انطلاق في سعينا نحو الكتابة، من المهمّ للغاية أن نفكّر في كلّ التناقضات والتوتّرات والتعدّديّة الّتي تحملها المعاني. عندما يتحدّث غسّان عن "كيفيّة" العودة، فإنّ البؤس والألم والدمار والأطراف المبتورة والمكسورة ستكون جزءًا من هذا الحوار.

دعينا نتروّى قليلًا لنفهم ضخامة الحدث الّذي نحاول وصفه. لقد غيّر ذلك اليوم من أكتوبر حياتنا جميعًا، وبشكل أبديّ. أتذكّر تمامًا أين كنت يومها - عندما استيقظت وفتحت هاتفي لأجد عددًا كبيرًا جدًّا من رسائلكِ. كنّا في مكانين وتوقيتين مختلفين، ولم يرفّ لكِ جفن، بينما تترقّبين صدور المزيد من الأخبار مع حلول الفجر. أعتقد وقتها أنّني خرجت وجلست تحت الشمس محاولة استيعاب ما يحدث، وكأنّني كنت بحاجة إلى رؤية يقين ضوئها الساطع، والإحساس بدفئها تحت جلدي لكي أثبّت هذه اللحظة، وأصدّق

أنّني لم أكن أحلم.

هل تتذكّرين كيف شعرتِ وقتها؟ وكأنّ سنوات عديدة قد مرّت منذ ذلك الحين. ما زلنا نستيقظ وننام على أخبار المجازر في غزّة يوميًا. أعود إلى مراجعة كلّ المشاهد والفيديوهات الّتي التُقِطَت لحظة كسر الحصار، وأحاول البحث عن الشمس. إنّها الشمس نفسها الّتي كنت أنظر إليها في تلك اللحظات، وأنا بعيدة عن البلد.

ما الّذي قصدتِه حين قلتِ إنّ الفلسطينيّين فتحوا الباب في ذلك اليوم من شهر أكتوبر — هي اللحظة الّتي قرّبتنا من طريق العودة وأبعدتنا عنّه في الوقت نفسه؟ أعتقد أنّني فهمتكِ إلى حدّ ما. لقد تبعث عمليّة فكّ الحصار حملات وحشيّة شرسة من الإبادة الجماعيّة المتسارعة الّتي يرتكبها مستعمرونا، والّتي أدّت إلى تدمير غزّة بشكل يمنعنا حتّى من التعرّف عليها، وأودت بحياة الآلاف من أبناء شعبنا. تبدو العودة بعيدة جدًّا في مقابل كمّ الخسارات الفادحة، وحتّى مع إدراكنا عظمة فعل العبور في ذلك الصباح المصيريّ. ولذلك، يبدو أنّ هناك تناقضًا في هذه المؤقّتيّة المزدوجة، فكرة القرب من فعل العودة والبعد عنه في الوقت نفسه. لنتذكّر لحظة اختراق البلدوزر السياج إلى الأمام كاسرًا الحصار. كيف يمكننا التعامل مع تلك اللحظة؟ بالنسبة لي، تبدو مفصلًا،

أو نقطة تحوّل
جاءت لفصل ما
قبل الحدث عمّا بعده،
وكالمفصل تمامًا
إمّا أن تدفعنا

تلك اللحظة بقوّة نحو مستقبل غامض، أو أن تُعيدنا إلى نقطة بداية العنف الاستعماريّ الّذي استقرّ في أرضنا. أتعلمين، ولا حتّى ذلك. أعتقد أنّنا في تلك اللحظة طُرِدنا جميعًا من إطار الزمن، ودخلنا مدار العودة. هذا الحيّز الّذي سنتجمّع فيه كلّنا في آن واحد، الفضاء المتناقض، الّذي ندفع أنفسنا فيه، ونتحرّك إلى الأمام من أجل أن نعود. هذا الحيّز تشكّل مع طردنا منذ عقود بشكل جماعيّ، حيث نعيش في مساحة وجوديّة تعمل ضمن مؤقّتيّة مختلفة، يتشابك فيها الماضي والحاضر والمستقبل للأبد.

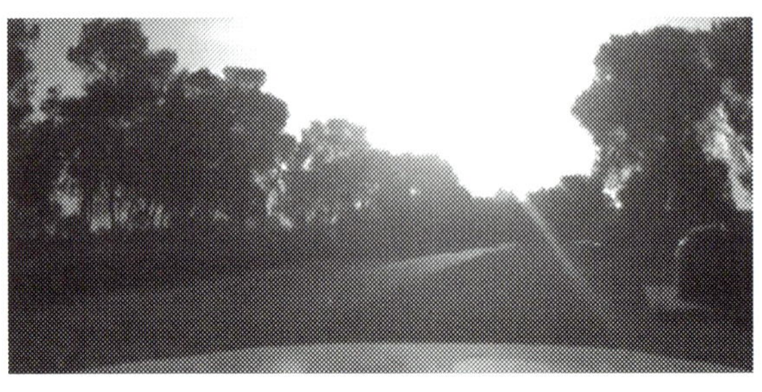

لست متأكّدة ما إذا كان كلامي منطقيًا، لذلك، دعيني أحاول مرّة ثانية.

أتعلمين كيف نتحدّث نحن الفلسطينيّين دائمًا عن العودة، وكأنّها حركة نتخيّل فيها الرجوع إلى استمراريّة حياتنا وأراضينا مثلما كانت قبل ١٩٤٨؟ وكأنّنا نعيش في متوالية زمنيّة، إذ نعلم أنّ الوقت يمضي إلى الأمام، ولكنّه يمضي نحو الزمن الّذي كنّا عليه في السابق، عندما كانت جغرافيّتنا واحدة، وكان بإمكاننا أن نستقلّ القطار من حيفا إلى بيروت. كيف يمكننا التعامل مع كلّ هذا التناقض؟ هل نمضي قدمًا لنعود بالزمن؟ ولهذا السبب، أعود باستمرار لاستعارة المدار؛ مدار العودة كحلقة —

نحن

نمضي

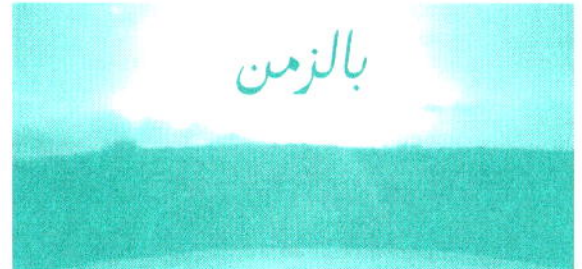

لنعود إلى

المكـــان

أعلم أنّ هذا الكلام غير منطقيّ، بل إنّه يعارض قواعد المنطق الأساسيّة، ولكنّنا لا ندور حاليًا في مجال العقلانيّة، إذ نحاول التعامل مع حركتنا عبر الزمان والمكان بطريقة تضمن مصداقيّة نضالنا. في هذا التمرين للخيال الراديكاليّ، نُقيم في الحلقة الخارجة عن المكان والزمان، وكأنّه تدريب على فعل عودة يستحقّ كلّ تضحياتنا الجماعيّة. إنّه لغز ميتافيزيقيّ، لأنّنا لا نلتزم بالقوانين الكونيّة الّتي تُملي علينا مفهوم "المضيّ قُدُمًا"، أي مرور الزمن بالمعنى الحرفيّ، ولا بالنبرة الاستعلائيّة الّتي تطالب بالقوّة فوق الحقّ.

من الممكن أن نفهم هذا الكلام إذا أعطيناه طابعًا بصريًّا. بالنسبة لي، يشبه مدار العودة دورة الأرض حول الشمس، إذ تدور حياتنا يوميًّا حول مسارات العودة، في معظم تفاصيلنا وممارساتنا اليوميّة.

مثل التسلّل إلى أراضي الـ٤٨ في الأيّام العاديّة
أو في مسيرات العودة
أو عند استرجاع أرشيفنا المنهوب
أو في جنازة شيرين.[٤]
عندما احتشد آلاف الفلسطينيّين عند باب الخليل، وتحرّرت القدس، ولو ليوم واحد فقط[٥] — لحظات التحرير العابرة هذه هي جزء من الدورات اليوميّة للعودة.

في هذا المدار، نلتقي أجدادنا حين كانوا صغارًا، كما سيلتقينا أولادنا عندما يكبرون. تقع مسارات العودة بين الماديّ والمتخيّل، إذ نتحرّك باستمرار بين هاتين الحالتين بشكل عابر. لقد نقَلَنا ذلك اليوم من أكتوبر من الحيّز الرمزيّ إلى حيّز الإمكانيّة، وفتح لنا هذا الجزء من الثانية الاحتمالات لتشكُّل أفق جديد وعالم مختلف. قد كانت فتحة من الجهة الوحيدة الممكنة، الجهة التي رفضت الاستسلام لمحاولات المحتلّين للسيطرة على المكان والزمان. وهذا وحده حدث جلل

٤. استشهِدت شيرين أبو عاقلة على يد قنّاصة إسرائيليّين أثناء تغطيتها لاقتحام الجيش لمخيم جنين للّاجئين في ١١ أيّار ٢٠٢٢.

٥. علي حبيب الله، في وداع شيرين... باب الخليل يُولَد من جديد، موقع متراس، ١٣ أيّار، ٢٠٢٢. https://shorturl.at/ld9ph

الجانب الّذي يرفض الاستسلام. أعتقد أنّ هذا التمييز مهمّ للغاية، خاصّة عندما نأخذ بعين الاعتبار الأدوات المفاهيميّة والماديّة الّتي تشكّل قوت عودتنا، تلك هي المكوّنات الأساسيّة الّتي تدور في فلك هذا المدار. ومع ذلك، فأنا لا أقصد وضع معنى نهائيّ ومحدود لمفهوم العودة. ما أستخلصه من شخصيّة سعيد، بطل رواية غسّان، هو مدى ضرورة فعل الرفض لمفهوم العودة. يُبدي غسّان رفضًا قاطعًا لفتح الأبواب عبر المفاوضات والتسويات الّتي تتنكّر على هيئة معاهدات سلام. هذا الشعور الجوهريّ بالرفض متأصّل في لغة غسّان عندما يقول سعيد: *"فحين فتحوها هم، بدا لي الأمر مرعبًا وسخيفًا وإلى حدّ كبير مهينًا تمامًا"*. تذكّرني هذه الجملة بفكرة "العائدين"، وهم الفلسطينيّون الّذين

عادوا مع ياسر عرفات كجزء من اتّفاقيّة أوسلو في عام ١٩٩٤.[٦] في تاريخنا، قام هذا الحدث بتعقيد مفهوم العودة، لأنّه كان نتيجة الخضوع السياسيّ، بمعنى أنّ ليست كلّ العودات متساوية. فإذا كانت العودة مسهّلة من قبل مضطهدينا ومشروطة بخضوعنا، فهي ليست العودة الّتي نريدها.[٧] لذلك، علينا السعي بثبات نحو عودة تليق بشعبنا، وتستحقّ التضحيات التي قدّمت على مرّ الزمن.

حين نذكر كلمة الرفض، فإنّنا نعني بها الموقف السياسيّ الّذي نتبنّاه، والمتجذّر في نظام من المعتقدات والأعراف الّتي تتبع ما نراه منطقيًا ومعقولًا. ومع ذلك، فإنّ لحظات الرفض الّتي نعود إليها مرارًا وتكرارًا تعبّر عن شيء آخر. ولكي أكون واضحة، فنحن لا نتحدّث هنا عن الإيماءات الاعتياديّة للرفض، كالمقاطعة مثلًا، بل عن كلّ تلك اللحظات العابرة والجريئة الّتي عرفها تاريخنا بشكل فعليّ، مثل كسر الحصار. تحدّثنا كثيرًا عن قدرة هذه اللحظات على التأثير فينا وتغييرنا، وذلك لأنّها غير منطقيّة أو مفهومة، وبكلّ بساطة، لأنّها استثنائيّة. أحاول التفكير في أبعاد أخرى لهذا الأمر، لأنّني أعلم، بل أشعر بأنّ خصوصيّة الرفض تحتاج منّا التوضيح.

بدأت الكتابة لكِ، وأنا متأكّدة من أهمّيّة وجود مفهوم الرفض في مدار العودة، ولكنّ الشكّ يملؤني؛ فمع كلّ محاولة لفهم جوهر الرفض، يفلت منّا دون قدرتنا على استيعابه. أتذكرين عندما سألتِني في إحدى المرّات عن الفرق بين الرفض والمقاومة؟ يجب أن أعترف لكِ بأنّني حتّى الآن لا أعرف الفرق. إنّه سؤال صعب ومثير للجدل، ولكن، وبما أنّنا نعتبر هذا التمرين الكتابيّ تدريبًا مسبقًا، فسوف أحاول التفكير فيه وتأمّله معك.

٦. يُقدّر عدد العائدين بين ٤٠ و١٠٠ ألف فلسطيني، ممّن استسلموا عند حل منظمة التحرير الفلسطينية، وتخلّوا عن النضال من أجل التحرير، واستبدلوا ذلك بمشروع بناء الدولة تحت مظلّة السلطة الفلسطينيّة.

٧. وفي الواقع، وكما عبّر غسّان، ينبغي أن نصل إلى المكان الذي نقول فيه إنّها عودة تُلغي نفسها. وأنّ الباب، حتّى وإن كان مفتوحًا، فهو لا يزال مغلقًا.

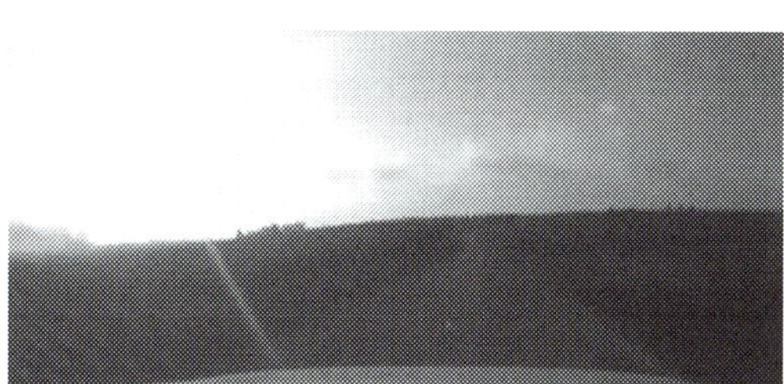

من الممكن التفكير في الأمر إذا ما عرّفنا الرفض كفعل مقاوم يحطّم الوضع القائم، ويفتح آفاقًا جديدة في الوقت نفسه، فهو ليس خاملًا ولا نتاج ردّ فعل، لكن في حالة المقاومة، فإنّ عنصر البقاء راسخ في الفعل، ويترتّب على ذلك الاستجابة إلى قيود الحاضر. ربّما يتميّز الرفض بكونه يحمل رؤية مستقبليّة؛ فالشخص يعبّر عن رفضه بعد إدراكه أنّ لديه خيارات أخرى.[٨] اسمعي، خطر لي سؤال؛ لماذا نسرح في هذا التمرين المفاهيميّ المجرّد؟ لطالما وجدتُ أنّ الممارسات الملموسة والفعليّة توفّر مساحة مثيرة أكثر للتفكير فيها.

دعيني أحاول مرّة أخرى، إذ أخاطب هنا الشهيد والأسير السابق[٩] والمفكّر وليد دقّة، من خلال أحد نصوصه الحديثة، 'السيطرة بالزمن'.[١٠] يحاول وليد أن يفهم ويشرح لنا لماذا يقرّر الأسير السياسيّ الخوض في تجربة الإضراب عن الطعام. يكتب وليد بدهشة أنّ مثل هذا القرار يناقض منطق العقل وقوانينه، فلماذا تعرّض جسدك للمعاناة في سبيل نضالك من أجل الحياة؟ ثمّ يستنتج أنّ دهشته تنبع من المنطق التحليليّ، أو البراغماتيّة، وحسابات أخرى لجدوى الفعل.

بالنسبة إلى الأسرى، وأولئك الذين ينخرطون في مثل هذه المساعي المضنية، فثمّة شيء آخر هام، وهو ما يسمّيه وليد 'المنطق العقلانيّ'، والذي يتجاوز ما هو معقول ومنطقيّ، ليشمل القلب والجسد والروح. إذ يكتب:

*"وهذه العقلانيّة لا تقرّ بحسابات العقل الّتي تكرّس الواقع، ولا تغيّره، وإنّما تأخذ الواقع الموضوعيّ وترتقي به. **ترفض**[١١] عقلانيّتهم النزول إلى الواقع، والبقاء هناك، وإنّما النزول بهدف الارتقاء إلى مصافّ أعلى. هذه العقلانيّة تشمل الاعتبارات الأخلاقيّة والقيميّة والإنسانيّة والوطنيّة العامّة، وقيم الذات الخاصّة، الّتي تحوّل العقل مع الجسد والقلب إلى أكثر من حاصل جمع ميكانيكيّ لمواجهة الاحتلال".*

٨.
لا نقول إنّ المقاومة والرفض منفصلان عن بعضهما - إذ يمكننا اعتبار الرفض جزء المقاومة الذي يحمل طابعًا أكثر تحديدًا.

٩.
أكره قول ذلك بهذه الطريقة، ولكنّ وليد لا يزال أسيرًا. إذ لا يزال جسده محتجزًا لدى الصهاينة الذين يرفضون تسليمه لعائلته حتى يتمكّنوا من دفنه ورثائه بشكلٍ لائق، ولن يسلّموا جثمانه حتّى يُنهي مدّة محكوميّته العام المقبل. هذه هي الممارسة الوحشيّة التي نسمّيها مقابر الأرقام.

١٠.
وليد دقّة، السيطرة بالزمن، أوان، ١٦ حزيران ٢٠٢١. https://www.awanmedia.net/article/6046

١١.
تأكيد قمنا بإضافته

←
(تُربِكُني هذه الفقرة).

كيف يمكن اعتبار منطق الأسير المضرب عن الطعام، والّذي يُخضِع جسده للجوع شكلًا من أشكال "النزول بهدف الارتقاء إلى مصافّ أعلى" كما يقول وليد؟ بينما يختفي الأسرى عن وجه الأرض، ويغيبون عن نسيج مجتمعاتهم، ويعيشون تحت وطأة السلطة الوحشيّة، إذ تُصَبّ عليهم كافّة أشكال العنف الممكنة دون رحمة، وإلى أجل غير مسمّى. في أضيق مساحة السجن، وعندما يسلب الأسير من كلّ عناصر التحكّم والسيطرة، يصبح الجسد آخر جبهة للمقاومة والمجال الأخير للتحكّم. لذلك، فإنّ كلّ فعل مقاوم يُقدِم عليه الأسير، يأخذ أبعادًا أكبر مهما كان بسيطًا، وتدهور جسد الأسير أثناء الاحتجاج يُعْلِي من شأن فعل المقاومة؛ إنّه فعل رفض يحمل في داخله قوّة تحافظ على الحياة والروح، لأنّه يحافظ على كيان روح الأسير باعتباره فردًا مستعمرًا، رغم انهيار جسده.

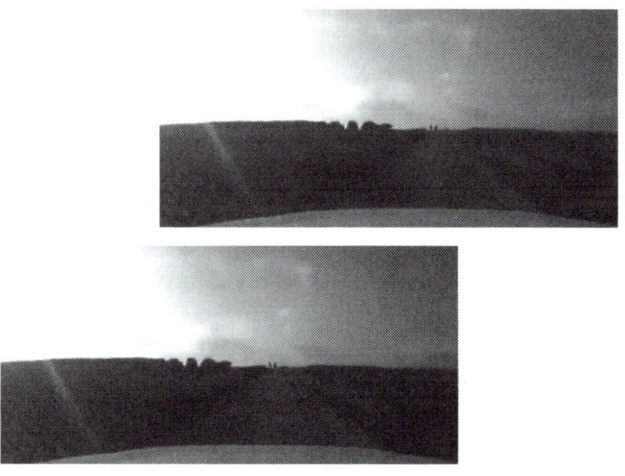

أعتقد أنّ هذا ما يعنيه وليد في حديثه عن المنطق الّذي يرفض كلّ الحسابات الاعتياديّة للجدوى والعقلانيّة، إذ يتوجّب علينا فهم ماهيّة الرفض، لا كردّ فعل، وإنّما كفعل مقاوم لفكرة الخمول والاعتياد، خاصّة إذا كنّا سنُقتل في نهاية المطاف. إنّه الجوهر الّذي يعترف بشكل أساسيّ بالحرب الوجوديّة الّتي تُشنّ علينا، ثمّ يحشدنا لرفض أساس الشروط والأحكام الّتي تجعل إبادتنا ممكنة طوال الوقت، وبشكل قاطع.

عندما يجلس رجل فوق أنقاض بيته ليشرب الشاي، ويدخّن ومعه أرجيلته، فإنّنا نعترف بهذا الفعل الرمزيّ كتحدٍّ وإنكار لسيطرة الصهاينة على زماننا ومكاننا. بالنسبة إلى أيّ مشاهد، فهو مجرّد رجل يجلس فوق الأنقاض، أمّا بالنسبة إلينا وإليه، فهذا مكانه ومنزله على أرضه، والّذي سيعيد بناءه في كلّ مرّة مهما تدمّر. هذا هو الرفض النموذجيّ.

لذلك من الضروريّ أن ننظر إلى كسر الحصار في ذلك اليوم من أكتوبر في ضوء ذلك كلّه — فهو جزء من مسار مقاومتنا الطويل الّذي لطالما سعى إلى صياغة شروطنا وأحكامنا، في مكاننا وزماننا، وحتّى في أغنياتنا ورقصاتنا. تتضمّن لحظة القطع هذه في جوهرها مفهومي الرفض والعودة، إذ إنّه رفض الاستسلام للحصار المفروض على غزّة منذ عقود، والمدعوم من قبل النظام العالميّ الّذي يعتبر حياتنا بلا قيمة، كما أنّ هذا الرفض هو شكل من أشكال العودة، حرفيًا ومجازيًا.[١٢] إذا كنّا سنحدّد مكانة هذه اللحظة في مدار العودة، فلن نمثّلها بخروج أو حياد عن المسار، بل بحركة كثيفة تشدّنا وتقرّبنا من جوهر نضالنا. في ذلك اليوم، كنّا أقرب ما نكون إلى الشمس

١٢. لم يبدأ هذا الرفض في ذلك اليوم من أكتوبر، ولم ينتهِ به. فكّروا في آلاف العائلات التي رفضت مغادرة منازلها في شماليّ غزّة خوفًا من تكرار مأساة النكبة. كذلك، أتذكّر مسيرة العودة الكبرى عام ٢٠١٨، حين أعلن أهل غزّة مرة أخرى رفضهم لكونهم لاجئين، وأصرّوا على حقّهم في العودة إلى منازلهم وأراضيهم التي هُجّروا منها عام ١٩٤٨.

عند الحديث عن الدوران حول الشمس والحركة نحو العودة، أودّ مشاركة ما يجول في خاطري، بينما نتأمّل في معاني وأفعال الرفض. صادف يوم الخامس عشر من أيّار ٢٠١١ ذكرى النكبة الثالثة والستّين، إذ كان وسيظلّ ذلك اليوم محوريًا في ذاكرتنا الجمعيّة. احتشد آلاف اللاجئين الفلسطينين عند حدود الأراضي الفلسطينيّة المحتلّة احتجاجًا على نفيهم الّذي طالت مدّته. سار بعضهم من الحدود السوريّة باتّجاه مجدل شمس في الجولان المحتلّ — وقُتِل هناك خمسة لاجئين برصاص القنّاصين الصهاينة، وقد تمكّن عدد قليل منهم وبشكل غير متوقّع اختراق الحدود وعبورها للوصول إلى قريتهم المحتلّة. ومن الجهة اللبنانيّة، شهدنا حركة مشابهة، إذ احتشد اللاجئون في قرية مارون الراس، وحاولوا العبور نحو فلسطين.

يومها أيضًا، قتلت قوّات الاحتلال عشرة متظاهرين، وفي اليوم نفسه، خرج مئات المتظاهرين إلى الشوارع في عمّان والقاهرة للمطالبة بحقّ العودة. وفي فلسطين، قلب القضيّة، أتذكّر بالتفاصيل تلك المظاهرات الشعبيّة في جميع أنحاء الوطن، إذ توافدت بعض جموع المتظاهرين نحو الحدود الشماليّة مع لبنان، بينما سار آخرون في حيفا والقدس وقلنديا ورام الله وغزّة. أعود بذاكرتي إلى ذلك اليوم بالتحديد، لأنّه يمثّل لحظة في تاريخنا تمكّنا من خلالها من خلخلة السرديّات الصهيونيّة وتعطيل مؤقّتيّاتها. إنّ القدرة الماديّة الّتي مكّنت اللاجئين من السير نحو حدود فلسطين، فتحت الباب من جهتنا، وغيّرت ذاكرتنا الجمعيّة، كما حوّلت مفهوم العودة من المجال الرمزيّ إلى الماديّ، وجعلت الأفق السياسيّ للتحرّر في متناول اليد.

كلّ هذا يعني أنّنا لا نستطيع مواصلة هذه المحادثة من دون تكريس المساحة والاهتمام لأهمّيّة الذاكرة الجمعيّة بالنسبة إلى مدار العودة، إذ يؤمن الفلسطينيّون بوجود رابط مقدّس يضمّ الذاكرة والوجود، وبالتالي العودة، ولهذا السبب يجب أن نتتبّع ونتأمّل بعض الآليّات التاريخيّة والهيكليّة الّتي تقع ضمن إطار هذه العلاقة.

أوّلًا — أعلم أنّ هذا سيبدو تبسيطًا للواقع، ولكن تحمّليني — لطالما انخرط المؤرّخون الفلسطينيّون والفنّانون الباحثون في الأدب وغيرهم في محاولات توثيق ذاكرتنا، واستعادة الأرشيف، وكشف 'الحقيقة'، إذ تهدف جهودهم إلى مواجهة السرديّة الاستعماريّة الاستيطانيّة الّتي تنكر حتّى وجودنا وعلاقتنا بوطننا، وتبرّر هذه السرديّة المشروع الاستعماريّ والتوسّعيّ في فلسطين. في الإطار الزمنيّ، تعتبر النكبة نقطة الانطلاق لمعظم هذه المساعي، وبالرغم من المجهود المهمّ، إلّا أنّه يجب علينا الكشف عن الطرق والأساليب الّتي نتناول من خلالها سؤال الذاكرة، لأنّنا لا نريد الوقوع في فخّ منطق الاستعمار الاستيطانيّ وأطر المحو الّتي يتّبعها.

دعيني أرجع خطوة إلى الوراء. عندما تكون النكبة نقطة الصفر الّتي نبني على أساسها ذاكرتنا وقصصنا حول النفي والسلب، وعند التعامل معها وكأنّها الحدث الجلل في تاريخنا، فإنّنا سنرضخ حتمًا لثنائيّة الهزيمة والنصر، وبالتّالي، سوف نستسلم لخطّيّة الزمن الّتي يفرضها علينا الاستعمار الاستيطانيّ في البدايات والنهايات، وسوف يقيّدنا منطق الفقد، ونبقى منغمسين في الماضي الكئيب، وأعتقد أنّ وليد قال: *"ولكنّني لا أريد العودة إلى فلسطين الماضي، فلسطين الانتدابيّة حيث الصبّار والرمّان وطواحين الماء، لأنّها ببساطة غير موجودة إلّا في الذاكرة"*[١٣] لهذا السبب. وهذا لا يمثّل إنكارًا للذاكرة، بل رفضًا أمام كلّ الركود والقيود الّتي تؤطّر الزمن والذاكرة، خاصّة عندما تصبح أسيرة حالة الحداد.

ثمّة جانب آخر يستدعي انتباهنا. عندما يقوم وجودنا على فكرة التوق إلى ماض فقدناه، فإنّنا بطريقة ما، نُقِرّ بالهزيمة المطلقة. أفكّر في عبدالرحيم الشيخ ورفضه لقراءة النكبة كهزيمة، إذ ينقد الإطار الّذي تُعَرَّف النكبة من خلاله، لأنّه يعلم أنّ هذا الإطار لازم لحماية المشروع الصهيونيّ وتعزيزه، وترسيخ بدايته على أنّها انتصار. يمكن لهذه النظرة التاريخيّة حجب كلّ اللحظات الدائمة والعابرة الّتي تمكّنا فيها من تشويه[١٤] الإطار الاستعماريّ الاستيطانيّ الصهيونيّ للزمان والمكان، مثل ذلك اليوم العظيم في ١٥ أيّار ٢٠١١. هذه اللحظات تُغذّي مخيالنا، وتدفعنا لتبنّي رؤية مغايرة وأكثر فعّاليّة للعودة والتحرّر.

١٣. عبد الرحيم الشيخ، "المكان الموازي: رسم الزمن في فكر وليد دقة"، مجلّة الدراسات الفلسطينيّة، العدد ١٣٥ (صيف ٢٠٢٣)، https://www.palestine-studies.org/ar/node/1653995

١٤. عبد الجواد عمر، "أشكال نازفة: ما بعد الانتفاضة"، مجلّة كريتيكال تايمز، آذار ٢٠٢٤، https://shorturl.at/jRXRu نستعير مفهوم "التشوّه" من وصف عبد الجواد عمر لكيفيّة تشويه أحداث مثل ٧ أكتوبر للزمانيّة والمكانيّة الصهيونيّة.

١٥.
رنا بركات، "النكبة مستمرّة والعودة مستمرّة"، لقاء نُشِر في مجلة جدليّة، ١٤ آذار ٢٠٢٤. https://www.jadaliyya.com/Details/45844

١٦.
آدم حاج يحيى، "مبدأ العودة: التقطيعة مع الزمن الصهيونيّ"، مجلّة بارابراكسيس، ٧ نيسان ٢٠٢٤.

عندما قلت إنّ مؤقّتيّة العودة توجد ضمن حاضر دائم، فإنّ هذا دقيق للغاية، وتحديدًا بسبب مركزيّة الذاكرة في وجودنا السياسيّ ونضالنا من أجل التحرّر. وفي بعض الأحيان، فإنّ تشبّثنا بالذاكرة شكل من أشكال العودة إلى الذات، وبدقّة أكثر، العودة إلى الذات الجمعيّة.

عندما نستشهد بأقوال كلّ من سبقونا، من جدّاتنا إلى شعرائنا إلى شهدائنا، فإنّنا نتلمّس في كلماتهم الدافع للحركة والمضيّ قدمًا لمجابهة هذا الركود، إذ نمارس مسارات عودتنا من مواقع التاريخ والذاكرة، سواء كانت أرضنا المقسّمة أو شعبنا المشتّت. تُطلق رنا بركات على هذا النهج في التعامل مع الذاكرة والتاريخ اسم 'العودة المستمرّة'،[١٥] وهي وسيلة أساسيّة تدعونا من خلالها لترسيخ عودتنا في الانتماء والحبّ، والإصرار على العلاقة الّتي تربطنا بأرضنا، وتحرير ذاكرتنا من أطر الاستعمار الاستيطانيّ— سواء كانت هيكليّة، زمنيّة، و/أو خطابيّة. لقد ذكّرني ما قالته رنا بجملة معبّرة كنت قد قرأتها في مقال آدم حاجّ يحيى،[١٦] والّذي تناول تساؤلات متعلّقة بالمؤقّتيّات والذاكرة والعودة، إذ يكتب: *"إنّ العودة تنتج الإمكانيّة وتحطّم الآليّة الّتي تقيّد مخيّلتنا وحياتنا. إنّها مدخل لمستقبل لا نهائيّ وحرّ".*

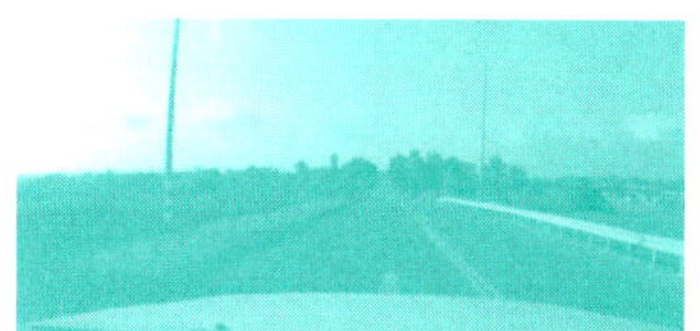

بالضبط، فكرة العودة كإمكانيّة، وأيضًا التفكير بها كحركة ومسار مستمرّين، يضمن لنا عدم الوقوع في الشعارات المستهلكة والكليشيهات المملّة حول ما تعنيه لنا الأرض والتحرّر. يشبه الأمر شخصيّة حمادة بطل قصّة 'عائد إلى يافا' لخالد عودة الله، الّذي يستمع إلى جدّه وهو يحكي قصص النكبة نفسها كلّ عام، فيشعر بالملل. هذا مقطع ممّا كتبه خالد بلغته وأسلوبه المميّز:

"ذابت كلمات الجدّ في الأثير، لكنّها دفعت حمادة كلّ عام شيئًا فشيئًا إلى تخوم هويّته المتشكّلة في فرن النكبة، وفي لحظة وعي مغامر، بدأ حمادة يقشّر عن ذاته "فلسطينيّته المنكوبة"، مثل برتقالة يافيّة وافية النضج في روايات جدّه، ليكتشف وهو يقشّر "فلسطينيّته" أنّه يقشّر في الوقت ذاته، صهيونيّة خفيّة مجدولة معها، فقد كانت فكرة "إسرائيل" قد تجوهرت في عادات الفكر للذهن المكلوم، خلايا عصبيّة، تمكّن الوعي من أن لا يكون إلّا ضدّه، فتحوّلت العودة إلى كلّ ما هو ضدّها، فمن عادات المغلوبين النزوع إلى التجريد بعد أن يوغلوا في الترميز.

لم تعد العودة في جهاز حمادة الإدراكيّ الجديد: مفتاحًا صدئًا، "كوشان" طابو، شعرًا عموديًّا أو حرًّا، فنًّا تشكيليًّا، حفل خطابة، صورًا بالأبيض والأسود، إحصائيّات وأرشيف "الأونروا"، وإنّما دفعه عقله الرياضيّ الصارم ونفوره من ألاعيب المجاز إلى تعريف العودة بـ"علم وتقنيّة عبور الحدود": أنواع الأسلاك الشائكة، أجهزة الرصد والمراقبة، جداول الدوريّات، أدوات الحفر والقطع، فنّ تمويه آثار الأرجل، معرفة أدلّاء الطرق ونقاط التهريب.

استحوذ عبور الحدود على حمادة اليافي، فلسطينيّ الأب مصريّ الأمّ، وصار العالم أمام عينيه حدودًا تنتظر أن تُعبَر..." [١٧]

١٧.
خالد عودة الله (@kodetalah)، "عائد إلى يافا"، منصّة إكس، ١٥ أيّار ٢٠٢٤.
https://encr.pw/yZ1yS

لـــــقد قرأت هذه القصّة القصيرة مرّات عديدة، واستوقفتني هذه الفقرة في كلّ مرّة، لأنّني أشعر برتابة مماثلة عند التفكير في مجازات العودة. كم من المفاتيح والخرائط سنحمل؟ عندما حوّل حمادة مفهوم الذاكرة إلى تقنيّة للعودة، جعلني أعيد التفكير في فهمي لها. كم منّا يحمل أفكارًا راسخة حول ديمومة السلطة وقوّتها، وبالتالي عجزنا الحتميّ في تفكيك هذه السلطة؟ لا أستطيع إلّا أن أفكّر في حمادة وفهمه لذاكرة النكبة على أنّها ضرورة اكتساب معرفة تقنيّة — شارات الطرق والجداول وأنواع الأسلاك الشائكة. ثمّة شيء هامّ للغاية في تركيبة الذاكرة إن نظرنا إليها كتقنيّات، إنّه تفعيل للمعنى من خلال الحركة على المستويين المفاهيمي والماديّ، وبالتّالي نحو العودة الفعليّة.

أريد أن نتأمّل قصّتي خالد وغسّان عن العودة، إذ إنّ رواية غسّان عن العودة مليئة بالندم، لذلك صاغها كقصّة تحاول لفت انتباهنا إلى أيّ جهة سيفتح الباب في طريقنا للعودة. أمّا في قصّة خالد، فيوضّح أن اعترافنا بالهزيمة الداخليّة ينتج سردًا جامدًا رمزيًّا مبنيًّا على كليشيهات العودة. وكيف حوّل وعي حمادة هذا السرد إلى طريقة يستطيع من خلالها اكتساب معرفة تقنيّة تؤهّله للعودة الفعليّة. يتحدّث كلّ من غسّان/سعيد وخالد/حمادة عن لحظات في تاريخنا تحدّد مسار نضالنا بطرق مختلفة. بين اعتقاد سعيد أنّ "كلّ الأبواب يجب ألّا تفتح إلّا من جهة واحدة، وأنّها إذا فتحت من الجهة الأخرى، فيجب اعتبارها مغلقة"، واعتقاد حمادة بأنّ "العالم صار أمام عينيه حدودًا تنتظر أن تُعْبَر". ما الّذي تغيّر؟ وهل ثمّة شيء تغيّر فعلًا؟

←
.١٨
حسين مروَة، الحزن القاتل والحزن المُقاتل، باب الواد، ٢ تموز ٢٠١٩.
https://shorturl.at/PTq5y

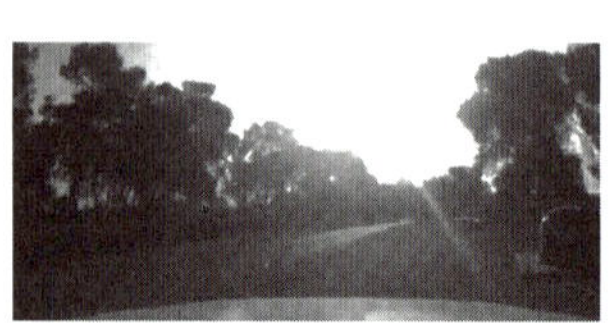

أخاف أن أفقد الرؤية. ثمّة أنهار من الدم وجبال من الأنقاض الممزوجة بلحم شعبنا. إذ إنّ الأسى كالهواء، ساكن وغير مرئيّ، بالرغم من وجوده. وأحيانًا يشتدّ فيصبح عنيفًا وشرسًا، كإعصار من الألم. لقد وصف حسين مروة هذا الأسى والحزن بكلمات ظلّت عالقة معي:

"إنّ حزنك هو الحزن القاتل، إنّه يقتلك أوّلًا، وإنّه -أوّلًا وآخرًا- قاتل من القتلة في صفّ العدوّ... إنّه يوجّه الرصاص، نفسيًّا ومعنويًّا، إلينا في معركة الصمود الّتي هي الآن عماد معركتنا الوطنيّة - القوميّة - الديمقراطيّة كلّها. وإنّ حزن «الفتى» في مكانه من المعركة ذاتها، هو الحزن المقاتل... إنّه الحزن المقدّس، إنّه «الحقد الشريف»... إنّه الشكل الأجمل والأنبل للحزن العظيم...".[١٨]

أسىً قاتل،

أسىً مقاتل،

أسىً مقدّس،

وكلّ العوالم والأكوان

التي تدور بينهم

لماذا توقظ العالم من النوم؟

*هذا ليس صوتي. هذا صوت ارتطام جثّتي بالأرض.

ولماذا لا تموت بهدوء؟

*لأنّ الموت الهادئ حياة ذليلة

والموت الصاخب؟

* قضيّة

هل جئت تُعلن حضورك؟

*بل جئت أُعلن غيابي[19]

تستيقظين في بعض الأيّام، لتقرأي حصيلة الشهداء، ثمّ تعودين إلى حـــالة التبلّد. وفي أيّام أخرى، تستيقظين وأنتِ تستصعبين حتّى الإحساس بجسدكِ، نتيجة المشاعر الفظيعة الّتي اجتاحتكِ بالكامل.[٢٠] لأكن صادقة، في الأسابيع الماضية وأثناء مراسلتنا، وجدت أنّني أشعر بثقل كبير، إذ دخلت كلماتنا حيّز الركود، ولم يتمكّن شيء من نفض هذا الثقل عن أكتافنا. أدركتُ أنّنا غرقنا من دون وعي بالتركيز على التفاصيل — أعتقد أنّها كانت طريقتنا للخوض في هذا الصمت المريب — حتّى تشتّت المعنى إلى شذرات مبعثرة.

→

١٩.
نودّ أن نشير هنا إلى فترة توقّف مراسلاتنا، والتي استمرّت لأيّام وأسابيع. تراجع زخم الكتابة تدريجيًا، وتوقّفت محاولاتنا لإحيائها، إذ كانت ثقيلة وغير سلسة. لذلك، توقّفنا وحاولنا تقييم ما أنتجناه حتّى تلك اللحظة.

٢٠.
نُعيد قراءة هذه الكلمات مرّة أخرى، ونحن نتلقّى أخبار مجزرة المواصي في ١٣ تموز، اليوم هو أحد تلك الأيّام، إذ نكتب هذه الكلمات حرفيًا في خضمّ المجزرة...

حاولنا في هذا النصّ أن نحلّل منطق العنف الاستعماريّ، وأن نتناول مفهومي المقاومة والرفض؛ كيف نفكّر تاريخيًّا ونتخيّل المستقبل، وكيف نتتبّع حركة ومسار العودة، وكلّ التشابكات الّتي تكوّنه. كيف يصبح إرثنا في الممارسة والفكر مركزًا محوريًّا في كتاباتنا وأشكال إنتاجنا للمعرفة. ترافق هذه الحركة أثمان لا تقدّر تهشّمنا جميعًا من الداخل، وتجرّنا نحو حالة غير محتملة مصيرها الغرق في بئر اليأس

إنّ الثمن هنا يقع على عاتق شهدائنا ودمائهم، نسرح ولو للحظة في أفكارنا عن المدارات والرفض والذاكرة... قبل أن يعلن الموتى غيابهم، ويجبرونا على التوقّف والإصغاء إلى الصمت الّذي يتسلّل عبر هذه السطور. يحوم مشهد الأجساد المهشّمة والبيوت المدمّرة فوق رؤوسنا ليخترق عظامنا ويستقرّ داخلها. أجد صعوبة في إدراك هذه الجزئيّة من مدار عودتنا. ماذا عن الشهداء؟ لقد أصبحوا كثرًا، إذ إنّ العدوّ لم يكتف بقتلهم فقط، بل حوّل أجسادهم إلى أشلاء لا يمكن التعرّف عليها. جبال من الأنقاض، والكثير من الجثث المتراكمة، جثث غمرها الركّام، وركام تغلغلت فيه الأشلاء، فامتزج أحدهما بالآخر، حتّى لم نعد نميّز اللحم من الحجر

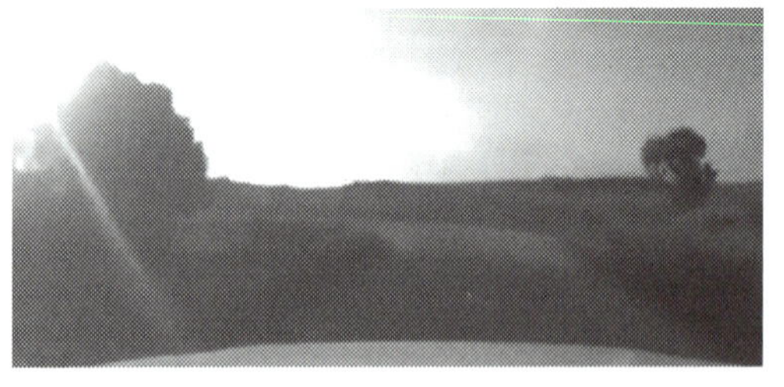

تُطاردني كلمات مريم الخطيب، وهي شاعرة من غزّة، حين كتبت:

"لا أحد يموت بجسد كامل، بعد الضربة الصاروخيّة، يبحث الجميع في الأنقاض محاولين تجميع أحبّائهم. تبحث الأمّهات عن رؤوس أطفالهنّ لكي يضعنها مع أجسادهم. أن تكوني أمًّا جيّدة في كافّة أنحاء العالم يعني أن توفّري لأولادك الطعام والدفء، ولكن لكي تكوني أمًّا جيّدة في غزّة، فعليكِ أن تدفني أولادكِ كاملين".[٢١]

٢١. مريم محمّد الخطيب. "ترف الموت"، معهد الدراسات الفلسطينيّة، ١٠ حزيران ٢٠٢٤، https://palestine-studies.org/en/node/1655709

بعد كتابة هذه الفقرة، لاحظت كيف شعر جسدي بالغثيان الذي أصبح بطريقة ما جزءًا منّي، إلى درجة أنني لم أعد أدرك أنّ هذا الشعور تحوّل إلى حالة شبه دائمة هذه الأيام. وكأنّ كرة معدنيّة ثقيلة تستقرّ في جوفي، تصدأ شيئًا فشيئًا.

يا لثقل هذه الكلمات، إنّ جلّ وثقل هذه اللحظة ليس فقط دماء شهدائنا، بل يمتدّ ليقطف أطرافهم الممزّقة ورؤوسهم المقطّعة. "صوت ارتطام جثّتي بالأرض"، إلا إنّ هذه الجثّة قد تشوّهت للأبد، وقسّم إعلان غيابها إلى عدّة صيحات، تصرخ جميعها في آن واحد — شقوق أزليّة — نلملمهم ليتمكّن عقلنا المحدود من استيعابهم — أجساد تحت الأنقاض، سلالات كاملة اختفت من السجلّ المدنيّ، وأحياء مُسِحت عن الوجود، بنية ومجتمع يتعرّضون للقصف بلا توقّف. نلملمهم لنتمكّن من استيعاب كلّ هذا. اتّسعت الفجوة، وأصبح الفراغ هاوية لا نجاة منها. الغياب ليس واحدًا، إذ لا نستطيع احتوائه. تستوقفنا الفجوات ويلتقطنا الفراغ، وعندما يعلن موتانا غيابهم، سنحملهم ونمضي، هذا هو جوهر كلّ شيء.

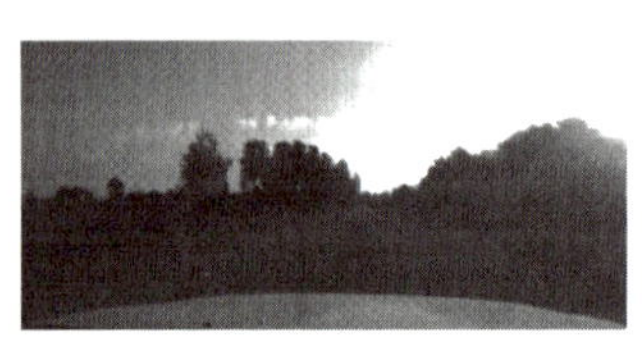

أعتقد أنّكِ تحاولين القول إنّنا بحاجة إلى تصوّر حركة من نوع مختلف، إذ تكلّمنا عن مدار العودة وكأنّ نضالنا يحدث ضمن إطار منظّم ومتكرّر. ولكن، ماذا لو بدلًا من سعينا لإيجاد منطق يسدّ هذه الفجوات، أن نفكّر بحركة تنشأ من داخل هذه الشقوق والشذرات الّتي تشكّل واقعنا. أفكّر في آخر فقرة كتبها غسّان في "ورقة إلى غزّة" حيث قال:

"يا صديقي.. أبداً لن أنسى ساق نادية المبتورة من أعلى الفخذ، لا، ولن أنسى الحزن الذي هيكل وجهها واندمج في تقاطيعه الحلوة إلى الأبد... لقد خرجت يومها من المستشفى إلى شوارع غزّة، وأنا أشدّ باحتقار صارخ على الجنيهين اللذين أحضرتهما معي لأعطيهما لنادية، كانت الشمس الساطعة تملأ الشوارع بلون الدم ... كانت غزّة، يا مصطفى، جديدة كلّ الجدة، أبدًا لم نرها هكذا أنا وأنت: الحجارة المركومة على أوّل حي الشجاعية، حيث كنّا نسكن، كان لها معنى كأنما وُضِعت هناك لتشرحه فقط، غزّة هذه، التي عشنا فيها ومع رجالها الطيّبين سبع سنوات في النكبة كانت شيئًا جديدًا، كانت تلوح لي أنّها... بداية فقط، لا أدري لماذا كنت أشعر أنّها بداية فقط، كنت أتخيّل أنّ الشارع الرئيسيّ، وأنا أسير فيه عائدًا إلى داري، لم يكن إلّا بداية صغيرة لشارع طويل طويل يصل إلى صفد، كلّ شيء كان في غزّة هذه ينتفض حزنًا على ساق نادية المبتورة من أعلى الفخذ، حزنًا لا يقف على حدود البكاء، إنّه التحدي، بل أكثر من ذلك، إنّه شيء يشبه استرداد الساق المبتورة".[٢٣]

٢٣. غسّان كنفاني، "ورقة من غزّة"، نُشرت مترجمة إلى الإنجليزيّة في كتاب "ثورة ١٩٣٦- ١٩٣٩في فلسطين" بواسطة الجمعيّة الثلاثيّة للقارّات في لندن عام ١٩٨٠. كُتب هذا النصّ في سياق الغزو الإسرائيليّ على غزّة ومجازر خان يونس ورفح في تشرين الثاني ١٩٥٦.

كما لو أنّ غسّان قد تنبأ باللحظة الّتي نعيشها اليوم عندما كتب هذه الفقرة. يحاول غسّان رسم صورة أساسيّة هنا — هذا المسار الوجوديّ الّذي يبدأ من غزّة، ويستمرّ إلى غاية استعادة الساق المبتورة. ثمّة شيء ما في هذا الخطّ الّذي يرسمه بين الطريق الّذي يبدأ من غزّة، ويسير نحو صفد، وفكرة استعادة الساق المبتورة، إذ يعطينا عبرة نحتاجها في مثل هذه اللحظة الّتي يعاني فيها الكثير منّا من الكسر والتشوّه. تخيّلي معي مسيرة العودة، نمشي على عكاكيز، بأطراف اصطناعيّة، نتحرّك ببطء ومن دون اتّزان أو ثبات، ولكنّنا نتحرّك معًا — هذا بالضبط ما أقصده بتخطّي الفجوة من داخلها. أريدنا أن نستحضر قليلًا هذا الغياب الّذي يخنقنا. لا نستطيع استعادة موتانا، وأُجبرنا في ظلّ ظروف الفصل الّتي فرضت علينا أن نشاهد إبادتنا ونحن على مسافة منها، وفي هذه اللحظة، تصبح الكتابة وسيطًا للتعبير عن الضعف الّذي نشعر به، والحسرة الّتي تملؤنا، ورغبتنا اللانهائيّة في احتضان أهلنا، واحتضان بعضنا البعض.

"ويا ريت عيني نهر يمي وشربن منّه"، لقد كنت أدندن هذه الكلمات طوال الأشهر العشرة الماضية بشكل لا شعوريّ. وكأنّها تهويدة تساعدني على تخفيف الألم. *"ويا ريت جسمي جسر يمي وقطعن عنّه"*.[٢٤] وما هي الكلمات الّتي تستطيع تخفيف ألم طرف مبتور أو حبيب قُتِل؟ لا يوجد أيّ منها. أتمنى لو كنت أستطيع أن أحتضن كلّ أب فقد ابنًا، وكلّ ابن فقد أمًّا. هذا هو شعوري تمامًا، رغبة ملحّة للمس، لأن أعانقهم. عند استحالة العناق، أتمنى لو أستطيع أن ألمسهم من خلال الكتابة. كيف يمكن أن أنقل تجربة اللمس هذه إلى اللغة؟ قالت هيباتيا: *"علينا أن نلمِس ونُلمَس عبر اللغة لنكون في هذا العالم."*[٢٥] الآن، لا يوجد عالم خارج غزّة، ونحن لسنا هناك. فكيف للّغة أن تصبح وسيلة لجعلنا أقرب.

٢٤. وِليَم نصّار، "على طريق عيتات"، ٢٠ تموز ٢٠١٣. https://www.youtube.com/watch?v=KbOnbjyDgxc

٢٥. فورلوميس، هيباتيا، "عشر أطروحات عن اللمس، أو كتابة اللمس". مجلّة نساء وأداء: عن النظريّة النسويّة، العدد ٢-٣ (٢٠١٤): ٢٣٢ - ٢٣٨

أعتقد أنّ ما تشير إليه هيباتيا هو التزام سياسيّ حول كيفيّة عيشنا في هذا العالم. تصبح اللغة في هذه الصيغة وسيطًا نسعى من خلاله للعيش، مناقضة بذلك الحدّ الّذي تتيحه لنا هياكل السلطة. لذلك، أرفض التسليم للمنطق المهيمن والقوانين العالميّة. نتحدّث عن مدارات خارج الزمان والمكان، وثورات تدور حول الشمس. نجوب في أرض غير مألوفة، لنستكشف الاحتمالات الموجودة في المكان الّذي نُفِينا إليه. أفكّر في أهمّيّة اللمس في اللغة — إذ يتجاوز التجريد، ويُصرّ على ما هو فعليّ، إذ إنّ جوهر اللمس هو شعورنا به، وهذه ليست استعارة. يمكن لذلك أن يتجسّد في تفاصيل الأشياء، بالضبط مثل وصفنا لدرجة حرارة الشمس، وشعورنا بأشعّتها عند ملامستها لجلدنا، ووقعها على أجسادنا. إنّ اللمس في اللغة هو أن ننتبه ونهتمّ ونراعي ونحبّ. كما أنّه رفض للفردانيّة؛ إذ إنّ من يَلمُس يُلمَس، وهكذا نكسر حقًّا حلقة الاغتراب. تكمن أهمّيّة اللمس في قدرته على استدعائنا للتجريب والشعور بشكل جماعيّ، أو كما يقول فريد موتن وستيفانو هارني: *"على الرغم من أنّنا نُجبر على أن نَلمُس ونُلمَس، وأن نشعر بالآخرين، ويشعر الآخرون بنا في حيّز اللامكان، وبالرغم من رفض الشعور والتاريخ والوطن، إلّا أنّنا نشعر (من أجل) بعضنا البعض".*[٢٦] يشمل حيّز اللامكان سفينة العبيد الّتي تعبر المحيط الأطلسيّ، كما يشمل مساحة الإقصاء الّتي يفرضها علينا عنف الحدود الاستعماريّة، عندما ينقضّ علينا بوحشيّة، ويطردنا إلى كافّة أرجاء الأرض. والسؤال هنا؛ كيف نشعر (من أجل) بعضنا؟ ولماذا يُعَدّ هذا مهمًّا، بل ضروريًّا، لبقائنا كشعب؟ يعرّف فريد وستيفانو نمط الإحساس هذا بالتلامس، أو *"القدرة على الإحساس من خلال الآخرين، كما يمكن للآخرين الإحساس من خلالك، أن تشعر بهم ويشعرون بك. إنّ هذا الإحساس بالمنفيّين، لا يخضع لدولة أو دين أو شعب أو حكومة أو قطعة أرض أو رمز".*[٢٧] يمكّننا هذا المجال من اللمس عبر اللغة والقدرة على الإحساس بالوجود، وتكوين العلاقات الحسّيّة والفعليّة مع أبناء شعبنا الّذين نحبّهم ولا نستطيع عناقهم جسديًّا. هو مجال راديكاليّ لأنّه يتحدّى أيّ تنظيم للسلطة. في هذا الحيّز المتبقّي من الحضور الحسّيّ الحرّ، علينا أن نُصرّ على إيجاد ممارسات بديلة لنتجاوز

٢٦.
ستيفانو هارني وفريد موتين، المشاع الخفي: التخطيط العابر والدراسات السوداء، (نيويورك: ماينر كوموزيشنز، ٢٠١٣): ٩٨-٩٩.

٢٧.
المرجع نفسه.

هذا الانفصال والشعور بالعزلة والاغتراب، وبالتالي ألّا نستسلم للمسافة الّتي فُرِضت علينا. ربّما تبدو هذه الأفكار غير مترابطة ومنفصلة عن الواقع.

↑

(في ذلك اليوم، بعد مجزرة المواصي، قال رجل على الشاشات: "خبّيت أولادي من الحرّ طول الطريق، وبسّ وصلنا، قتلوهم").

↓

لا أعلم كيف أتابع بعد أن وصلنا إلى هنا. أفكّر فقط في بحر الكسور الّذي غمرنا، وفي السؤال المتعلّق بكيفيّة نجاتنا من هذه الإبادة. في صلب التفكير بالإحساس واللمس كممارسات تخيّليّة تستطيع أن تسعفنا في هذه اللحظة، يكمن اليأس من الاستسلام للألم كمقبرة حتميّة حيث تموت كافّة حواسّنا. ولكن بدلًا من ذلك، علينا تحويل هذا الأسى إلى توتّر يرافقنا باستمرار، مثل نار لا يمكن إطفاؤها أبدًا.

هذا هو الأسى المقدّس والمقاتل.

نعم، يجب أن نعترف بالمسافة الّتي تفصلنا، والأمان الذي تمنحنا إيّاه، وحتّى بشعور الامتياز الّذي يحتلّنا عند كتابة هذه الكلمات. هذا تحمّل للمسؤوليّة. من المستحيل إيجاد الكلمات المناسبة، أو أيّ كلمات على الإطلاق. ولهذا، سيبقى هذا النصّ غير مكتمل. بما أنّنا في آخر هذه المحادثة، فإنّ رؤيتنا الّتي رسمناها لمدار العودة، مشوّهة أيضًا. ليس لأنّ مسارات العودة الّتي تصوّرناها لا تعمل، ولكنّها لا تدور حسب منطق الأرقام الّتي تدور على أساسها الكواكب. إنّ كلّ العناصر موجودة — الرفض، الذاكرة، التضحية والأسى — ولكنّها لا تتحرّك بتناغم، وليست عناصر منهجيّة تتّحد لتشكّل كيانًا واحدًا. لا، عندما يكون لهذا المدار الكوني مسار مغلق ومحدّد، ستكون رحلة عودتنا متعرّجة، ذات حوافّ حادّة وصدوع، هوّات عميقة وطرق مفخّخة، مرصوفة بأجساد شهدائنا وأطراف مُصابينا، ومحاطة بسنين أُهدرت في زنازين السجون، أو في الانتظار على الحواجز، بينما يغلق المدار في دورته الثابتة، حيث تنتظم الكواكب على مسارها دون أن تضلّ الطريق، إنّ حركة ومسار عودتنا شيء لا يمكن توقّعه، فهو مفتوح للارتجال، وهو ليس نتاج جمع أجزاء منطقيّة، لأنّ لديه منطقه العقلانيّ الخاصّ، كما قال وليد، ومع ذلك، فالقول إنّ العودة غير متوقّعة لا يعني أنّها تفتقد لليقين، بل على العكس تمامًا، إذ نؤمن بأنّها قائمة على اليقين، حتّى وإن كانت تتحدّى منطق السلطة، أو "الحقائق على الأرض". نحن نؤمن بها كيقين الشمس الساطعة ودفئها الّذي يغمرنا. تمامًا مثل ذلك اليوم، عند ساعات الصباح الباكر، حين حبس العالم أنفاسه وهو ينتظر تكشّف الأحداث.

أتذكرين كيف شعرتِ؟ كانت الشمس ساطعة،
وازداد توهّجها حتّى غمرت أرواحنا بالدفء،
قبل أن تحرقنا بلمستها.